Inhabiting the Church

Inhabiting the Church

Biblical Wisdom for a New Monasticism

JON STOCK, TIM OTTO, AND
JONATHAN WILSON-HARTGROVE

Cascade Books
A division of *Wipf & Stock Publishers*
199 West 8th Avenue, Suite 3 • Eugene OR 97401

INHABITING THE CHURCH
Biblical Wisdom for a New Monasticism

ISBN 10: 1-59752-990-7
ISBN 13: 978-1-59752-990-7

Cataloging-in-Publication data

Stock, Jon.
Inhabiting the church : biblical wisdom for a new monasticism / Jon Stock, Tim Otto, and Jonathan Wilson-Hartgrove.

x + 130 p. ; 23 cm.

Eugene, Ore.: Cascade Books

ISBN 10: 1-59752-990-7   (alk. paper)
ISBN 13: 978-1-59752-990-7

1. Community—religious aspects—Christianity. 2. Benedict, Saint, Abbot of Monte Cassino. Regula. 3. Benedictines—Rules. 4. Monasticism and religious orders—Rules. 5. Christian life. I. Title.

BV4518 S76 2007

Manufactured in the U.S.A.

Contents

Foreword / vii
Acknowledgments / ix
Introduction / 1

1

Vows

Jon Stock / 7

2

Conversion

Jonathan Wilson-Hartgrove / 27

3

Obedience

Tim Otto / 57

4

Stability

Jon Stock / 87

Conclusion / 119
Abbreviations / 123
Bibliography / 125

Foreword

CONVERSATIONS BETWEEN CONTEMPORARY CHRISTIAN communities and Benedictine monasticism are among the most surprising and promising in the church today. Given that the roots of monasticism and of contemporary Protestantism lie in different parts of the Christian tradition, mutual engagement between contemporary Christians and monastics has been rare. Recently, however, the scene has shifted, and *Inhabiting the Church* represents the new eagerness to learn the art of living together faithfully from experienced and ancient practitioners.

Today, many Christians long for more vibrant community, and yet most of us lack the requisite skills and practices. With our wariness of vows and commitments, and our individualistic and mobile lifestyles, we are not very good candidates for community life. And yet, life in community is central to Christian identity, purpose, and ministry in the world.

Benedict's understanding of what makes Christian community both possible and good was shaped centuries ago in a social and cultural context very different from our own. Nevertheless, the wisdom of this community founder, the continuing fruitfulness of living under the Benedictine rule, and the centuries-long experience of the Benedictine tradition continue to speak.

Tim Otto, Jon Stock, and Jonathan Wilson-Hartgrove share a commitment to living in community. They are practitioners who are also deeply appreciative of the wisdom of those who have gone before us. Shaped by free-church Protestantism and fascinated with Benedictine monasticism, they are looking for a richer Christian spirituality and a more robust practice of community.

Through serious biblical engagement with central features of Benedictine life—life under a rule, life lived in commitment to a particular people and place, obedience, and ongoing conversion—the authors challenge readers to a deeper faithfulness and offer a way to think about Christian discipleship that is simultaneously ancient and fresh.

Efforts at a sustained communal life among Christians are often dismissed as idealistic and naïve, something folks will outgrow once they see how hard or "impractical" it is. But those who allow grace and fidelity to shape their communities, and those who keep Christ at the center, show us that it is possible to live out a form of discipleship that embraces the startling, life-giving and uncomfortable claims of Jesus on us, our practices, and our relationships.

With careful biblical reflection and nuanced application, the authors demonstrate that Benedictine wisdom might be opened up more widely to the *new monasticism* or those Christians currently living in or forming intentional communities. But the more far-reaching desire of the writers of *Inhabiting the Church* is that this lively convergence of countercultural commitments and lifestyles speaks a word of help, encouragement, and challenge to the larger church. Though the number of Christians living in intentional communities is comparatively small, their voices are important and illuminating for more conventional congregations whose members want a deeper discipleship and a more vibrant community.

Christians yearn for a way of life that is whole and holy, a form of life that is rooted in Christ and deeply connected with others, and yet we struggle to imagine what that might look like in our time and place. The authors of this book offer some important suggestions, and offer them with humility, hope, and wisdom.

Christine D. Pohl
Professor of Social Ethics
Asbury Theological Seminary
Wilmore, Kentucky
Author of *Making Room:*
   Recovering Hospitality as a Christian Tradition

Acknowledgments

WE WOULD LIKE TO say thanks, first of all, to Benedictine brothers and sisters who have shared their wisdom with us, especially to Sister Mary Forman of St. Gertrude's Monastery in Cottonwood, Idaho, and Sister Mary Elizabeth Mason from Annunciation Monastery in Bismarck, North Dakota—both of whom read the manuscript and gave helpful feedback (along with copies of Benedictine sources that we had no access to). Thanks also to St. John's Abbey in Collegeville, Minnesota, and to St. Benedict Monastery in St. Joseph, Minnesota, who hosted Jonathan at their Monastic Institute and engaged in lively conversation about what the new and old monastics have to learn from each other. We look forward to more conversation and time together.

Others also read and helped shape our thoughts in these chapters. We'd like especially to thank Steve Fowl, Jonathan Wilson, Christine Pohl, Fred Bahnson, Sarah Jobe, Shane Claiborne, Steve Long, Kent McDougal, Brian Logan, Dave Cheuvront, Barry Harvey, Zoe Mullery, Eric Olson-Getty, Matt Gates, Jeremy Alder, and Tim McGee.

Finally, we want to thank our communities: Church of the Sojourners, Church of the Servant King, and Rutba House. Without you, these words not only would never have been written; they would also be empty. In a similar way, our lives happen and find their meaning in your midst. You are the body of Christ to us.

Tim Otto
Jon Stock
Jonathan Wilson-Hartgrove

Introduction

THIS BOOK IS A collection of biblical–theological reflections on the three-fold Benedictine vow of obedience, conversion (or *conversatio*), and stability. Benedict is considered the father of Western monasticism. We know little about his life except that after some time as a hermit, he established multiple monasteries and authored the monastic rule of life known as the *Rule of St. Benedict.* Through the centuries, distinct Benedictine congregations have been instruments of reform, despite Papal attempts to centralize the movement. For instance, Benedictines are largely responsible for maintaining order and culture after the fall of the Roman Empire. The Reformation curtailed the activity and influence of Benedictines; they found their properties seized in northern Europe and in the British Isles. But in the nineteenth century, Benedictines experienced a remarkable revival of the Rule in both Europe and America. The Benedictines are known especially for their hospitality, education, and charity. Today, Benedictine abbeys are autonomous but grouped in congregations, which together form a confederation.

That's enough history to suggest Benedict's importance, but this is neither a book on Benedict of Nursia nor a historical work on Benedictine monasticism. The authors of this volume are not Benedictines. We are part of an eclectic lot that have adopted to varying degrees the label "new monasticism."[1] Our origins are primarily in free-church Protestantism, and our communities do not often look much like traditional monasticism. We stole the term "new monasticism" from our friend Jonathan Wilson and from his theological reflection on the work of Alasdair MacIntyre.

Alasdair MacIntyre closes his seminal work *After Virtue* drawing a parallel of sorts between our age and the last days of the Roman Empire.

---

[1] See Rutba House, *School(s) for Conversion.* New monasticism has been featured in cover stories by both *Christianity Today* (September 2005) and *The Christian Century* (October 18, 2005). For more information, see http://www.newmonasticism.org.

It is always dangerous to draw too precise parallels between one historical period and another; and among the most misleading of such parallels are those which have been drawn between our own age in Europe and North America and the epoch in which the Roman empire declined into the Dark Ages. Nonetheless certain parallels there are. A crucial turning point in that earlier history occurred when men and women of good will turned aside from the task of shoring up the Roman *imperium* and ceased to identify the continuation of civility and moral community with the maintenance of that *imperium*. What they set themselves to achieve instead—often not recognizing fully what they were doing—was the construction of new forms of community within which the moral life could be sustained so that both morality and civility might survive the coming ages of barbarism and darkness. If my account of our moral condition is correct, we ought also to conclude that for some time now we too have reached that turning point. What matters at this stage is the construction of local forms of community within which civility and the intellectual and moral life can be sustained through the new dark ages which are already upon us. And if the tradition of the virtues was able to survive the horrors of the last dark ages, we are not entirely without grounds for hope. This time however the barbarians are not waiting beyond the frontiers; they have already been governing us for quite some time. And it is our lack of consciousness of this that constitutes our predicament. We are waiting not for a Godot, but for another—doubtless very different—St. Benedict.[2]

Wilson, in his book *Living Faithfully in a Fragmented World*, closes with a reflection on this "prayer" of MacIntyre's for a new Benedict. Wilson calls for a new monasticism that "will, doubtless, be a very different form of life."[3] He suggests four characteristics of a new monasticism:

1. A recovery of the gospel *telos* that sees the whole of life under the lordship of Jesus Christ. This recovery will blur the distinction between sacred and secular.

[2] MacIntyre, *After Virtue*, 263.
[3] Wilson, *Living Faithfully*, 72

2. It will be for the whole people of God. It will not divide the people of God into "religious" and "secular" vocations.

3. It will be *disciplined*. This is necessary because the recovery of the gospel *telos* will not come easily or quickly. However, because this discipline will be for the whole people of God, it cannot simply be a recovery of the old monastic rules. The disciplines are always only a means to an end—the faithful life and witness of the church (and we must never get our ends and means confused. Means must always be consistent with the ends and must never submit to principles of utility or to the ends of the aesthete, the manager, or the therapist.).

4. It will be undergirded by deep theological reflection and commitment. The purpose of the new monasticism is to provide the church with a means to recover its life and witness in the world. The new monasticism provides a means by which an undisciplined and unfaithful church may recover the discipline and faithfulness necessary for its mission in the world. Right theology will not of itself produce a faithful church. A faithful church is marked by the faithful carrying out of the mission given to the church by God in Jesus Christ, but that mission can be identified only by faithful theology. So, in the new monasticism we must strive simultaneously for a recovery of right belief and right practice.[4]

Wilson understands that small communities of discipleship existed but were few and far between. It was his assessment that more needed to be done:

> . . . this new monasticism is what we are called to by my use of MacIntyre to analyze the life of the church in our fragmented culture . . . we are constantly tempted to form a church that will simply undergird the civil order. A new monasticism refuses that temptation. Given our fragmented world, the church is constantly tempted to import that fragmentation into its life. A new monasticism seeks to heal that fragmentation by rediscovering the *telos* of human life revealed in the gospel. . . . The new monasticism envisioned here is the form

[4] Ibid., 72–76

by which the church will recover its *telos*, the living tradition of the gospel, the practices and virtues that sustain that faithfulness, and the community marked by faithful living in a fragmented world.[5]

In the summer of 2004, the folks at the Rutba House in Durham, North Carolina, invited a group of practitioners, scholars, and dreamers together to consider what this new monasticism might be all about. The goal was to pull together a working group in order to write a rule for living for the new monasticism. We heard from one another about challenges that were being addressed within different communities and the particular practices that had been developed to address them. While a new rule was not written, we were able to suggest twelve marks of a new monasticism. The book *School(s) for Conversion: 12 Marks of a New Monasticism* was a product of this conference.

Early in the conference, Michael Cartwright, from the University of Indianapolis, called new monasticism into a conversation with the "old monasticism." Parker Palmer and others in the 1980s sought a movement similar to the new monasticism, he said, but jettisoned the experience and wisdom of the old. Cartwright's own experience in the St. Brigid of Kildare consultations between United Methodists and Benedictines has led him to believe that much can be learned from patient engagement with old monasticism. He warned against the "commodification of experience" that is a temptation for Protestants shaped by a consumer culture—that we might "shop for the best of Catholicism" and then move on to other markets. Commitment to conversation with the other as "other," Cartwright said, makes it possible for us to understand ourselves differently while remaining true to our own convictions.

Cartwright's exhortation is difficult to heed. How is it that we might resist a commodification of old monasticism and still remain true to our own convictions? This is our first attempt to engage the "other" monasticism. Our attempt may be fraught with error. We suspect that time and practice will be the only apologies for whether or not we have been true to our dialogue partner and to our own identity.

[5] Ibid., 78.

Regardless, armed with a conviction that engagement was needed, we decided to engage the Benedictine vows, and this volume was birthed. Why did we decide to engage the Benedictine vows? The flippant answer is that "we had to start somewhere!" A more considered reflection points to the 1500-year Benedictine existence and to their great missionary and educational work. This order has in its ranks Gregory the Great, Hilda of Whitby, Augustine of Canterbury, Hrothswitha, Anselm, Heloise, Bernard of Clairvaux, Hildegard of Bingen, Bede, Gertrud of Helfta, Boniface (the Apostle of Germany), Leoba, and Alcuin—among many others. Certainly, we can learn something interacting with them.

Joan Chittister's *Wisdom Distilled from the Daily: Living the Rule of St. Benedict Today* is an excellent introduction to the Rule of St. Benedict for the modern outsider. While some consider the work too pedantic or too political, we have gained plenty of insight reading the book, and a greater appreciation for Benedictine life. The volume you are now reading is really nothing like Chittister's volume. We are not yet on our way to becoming Benedictines. This book is merely an attempt to learn, to imagine, from our own social locations, how Benedict's wisdom might speak to the church.

We came asking the question, did Benedict get it right? We decided to use his central vow as a springboard for a biblical–theological reflection that was true to our own free-church Biblicist roots. To some degree, what shapes this book is mere intuition. Benedict must have done something right. It may be that our own reflections on the vow differ substantially from the Benedictine self-understanding. But it is our hope that new monastic communities will benefit from Benedictine wisdom. Obedience, conversion, and stability have not been a part of our larger dialogue.

This book has been written by breaking up the Benedictine vow into its three components. Each component has been addressed by a different author. While this was a very practical way to proceed, it is not without its faults, the largest of which is the false impression that these three elements are distinct vows in and of themselves within Benedictine faith and practice. The Benedictines tell us otherwise. And our own experience concurs. While these three components can be distinguished for the sake of clarity, they cannot stand on their own. This is, we admit, something of a mystery. But Christians are at least accustomed to mysteries in which three are one.

We invite you to consider the mystery with us in faith and in practice.

Tim Otto
Jon Stock
Jonathan Wilson-Hartgrove

I

Vows

Jon Stock

On the Legitimacy of Vows

HISTORICALLY, MONASTIC VOWS HAVE taken a beating since the Reformation. My Protestant heritage takes a dim view of any type of discipline that would seem to embrace legalism or justification by works, that would undercut the concept of the priesthood of all believers, or that would call Christians to a practice that may violate the principle of *sola scriptura*.

In America in an era when even marriage vows are often only taken seriously at the moment and may be cast aside if we are failing at self-actualization, the suspicion of monastic vows is even greater. Much is made of how we are shaped by late capitalism and by our market-driven economy, and those are legitimate issues of concern. We are trained to consume. We have been taught that true freedom is the freedom of consumer choice; it is the freedom to seek new alternatives that fulfill our immediate felt needs. Disney taught us as children that the greatest good is to follow our dreams, and that it is legitimate to betray our communities or to abandon our teammates in order to realize our dreams.[1] Madison Avenue has taught us that we've got to conform to the right body type and keep up with the latest fashions in order to find love and acceptance. Wall Street has instructed us that our own economic security is tied up with our continued consumption. The entire system is built upon the necessity of an autonomous self who is able to re-create itself at a moment's notice.[2]

---

[1] *The Little Mermaid* and *Little Giants* are two good examples of movies that teach us to justify the pursuit of "dreams" over against the good of the community. Unfortunately, there are plenty of other media examples.

[2] I recommend Clapp, "Theology of Consumption." Other resources include Hauerwas, *Better Hope*; Bartholomew and Moritz, *Christ and Consumerism*; Beaudoin, *Consuming Faith*; McDaniel, *Living from the Center*; Schut, *Simpler*

I am a free-church Protestant born in the Western United States where we don't like anyone telling us what to do. Groups of Christians who make vows together and keep them are a tremendous threat to our way of life. But the Protestant in me forces me to ask: is the making of vows biblical? The purpose of this chapter is to allow the ancient text invade our time and space and give consideration to the biblical witness regarding the making and keeping of vows or promises.

In conducting biblical investigation, it is always important to keep in mind just how big of a difference there is between a twenty-first century Oregonian and the ancient near east. In fact, one finds vows not only in the Bible, but in the inscriptions and literatures of virtually all peoples in the ancient Mediterranean—from Babylonians and Assyrians to Greek and Romans. Why was the vow so prevalent in these societies? They shared a number of basic characteristics and values. Most important for our purposes, they were all honor–shame societies and their populations lived predominantly in villages (that is, in close, face-to-face contact). The making of a vow was the public engagement of a person's honor. If he or she did not keep the vow, the community held that person accountable—the one making the vow opened herself or himself up to public loss of honor.[3] As classical monasticism developed—both in Europe and Egypt—the monks, nuns, and friars were also living in face-to-face communities to which they were accountable. As we read these ancient texts, it is essential that we not lose this element of face-to-face. We must ask whether or not any of the vows discussed in this book can be actually practiced without a similar social construction. In a day and age that offers us internet "church" and a plethora of virtual communities—we must be wary of divorcing the following texts from their contemporary social structure. If vows are applicable for new monasticism, they can only be such in a setting where face-to-face encounter is a daily reality. I suspect that vows, ultimately, are only as true as the life together that they represent. If new monasticism has any parallel with these ancient societies it is, that despite individualistic Western life, they live in close proximity and are daily accountable to one another.

Living; and Dawn, *Unfettered Hope*.

[3] Malina, *The New Testament World*; on vows, 41; on honor and shame generally, see 27–57.

Biblical and Theological Considerations

This essay is most certainly not a work of academic theology, but any essay of this nature is bound to be rife with theological presuppositions. I want to start by mentioning a few presuppositions that are key to the argument of this chapter:

1. Jesus is the God-bearer; this means that what we can know of God, we see in Jesus: "he who sees me sees him who sent me" (John 12:45).

2. As followers of Jesus, we are called to bear witness to the character of God. We are called to be holy as God is holy. We are called to be perfect as our heavenly Father is perfect. The religious temptation is to take these biblical calls to holiness and perfection and replace them with our own visions of "holiness" or "perfection" (usually some type of culture-bound moral code which, upon accomplishment, guarantees our personal salvation). It is God, in God's own being and agency, who gives definition to a Christian understanding of "holiness" or "perfection."[4]

3. It is a primary task of the people of God to discern who God is and what God is doing and then to bear witness to this God for the sake of the world.

This is not to say that speaking of God is unproblematic—we are human and quite limited in our ability to utter anything about God. "As ministers we ought to speak of God. We are human, however, and so cannot speak of God. We ought therefore to recognized both our obligation and our inability and by that very recognition give God the glory. This is our perplexity."[5] Again, as noted above, the key to our recognizing God is God's activity in the world. We can only speak of God in relation to his agency, and we are very dependent upon metaphors. For example, to call God a *faithful spouse* to Israel is merely to employ a metaphor, but a metaphor that is grounded in the steadfast action of Yahweh.

---

[4] See Deut 10:12–22, especially vv. 17–19. Israel is enjoined to imitate its God.

[5] Barth, *Word of God,* 186.

Old Testament Considerations

1. Israel offers substantial testimony that Yahweh is a God who makes promises and creates covenants.[6]

Yahweh is a covenanting God. The family narratives of Genesis 12–50 lay the foundation of Yahweh's covenantal vision for creating community.

> Now the Lord said to Abram, "Go from your country and your kindred and your father's house to the land that I will show you. And I will make you a great nation, and I will bless you and make your name great, so that you will be a blessing. I will bless those who bless you, and him who curses you I will curse; and by you all the families of the earth shall bless themselves. . . . Then the Lord appeared to Abram, and said 'to your descendants I will give this land. . . ."
> (Gen 12:1–3; 12:7)

The creation of a community that will be a blessing to all the families of the earth requires people and a place to begin; Yahweh comes to Abram and promises both. This promise is reiterated in Genesis 13:14–17 after Abram and Lot separate (Lot setting up his tent near Sodom). Yahweh's intent in calling Abraham is nothing short of the "re-forming of creation, the transforming of the nations."[7] Genesis 1–11 unfolds a story of a world gone awry. With the covenantal call of Abram, Yahweh begins setting things right.

In Genesis 15, Abram becomes anxious over his lack of an heir, noting that Eliezer of Damascus, a slave in his house, will become heir. Yahweh promises "this man will not be your heir; your own son shall be your heir" (Gen 15:4). Yahweh takes Abram outside and says to him, "Look toward heaven, and number the stars, if you are able to number them. . . . So shall your descendants be" (Gen 15:5). Abram

---

[6] Key studies on this theme include Alt, "God of the Fathers," 1–77; Westermann, *Promise to the Fathers*; Mendenhall, *Law and Covenant*; and Baltzer, *Covenant Formulary*. The classic Old Testament theology that presents covenant as a central paradigm is Eichrodt, *Theology of the Old Testament*. The theme of "promise" plays an important role in Gerhard von Rad's work. I am greatly indebted to Walter Brueggemann, particularly to his "Covenant as a Subversive Paradigm," and to his *Theology of the Old Testament*.

[7] Brueggemann, *Genesis*, 105.

believes Yahweh, and it is reckoned to him as righteousness (Gen 15:6). Yet, Abram wants assurance of Yahweh's promise. Yahweh responds by instructing Abram to cut in two a heifer, a female goat, and a ram, laying the halves over against each other, along with a slaughtered turtledove and a pigeon. Abram falls into a deep sleep, during which he is given a foretelling of the slavery in Egypt and the liberation back into the Promised Land.

> When the sun had gone down and it was dark, behold a smoking fire pot and a flaming torch passed between these pieces. On that day the Lord made a covenant with Abram, saying, "To your descendants I give this land, from the river of Egypt to the great river, the river Euphrates, the land of the Kenites, the Kenizzites, the Kadmointes, the Hittites, the Perizzites, the Rephaim, the Amorites, the Canaanites, the Girgashites and the Jebusites. (Gen 15:17–20)

Here, in a scene similar to that of Jeremiah 34:18 (another reference to an animal divided in half), a covenant is ratified as those who are party to the covenant pass between the slaughtered animals, in effect declaring that they accept a similar slaughter if they break the covenant. Walking along this sacrificial pathway is a symbolic action enacting not only the covenant's promise of land but also a curse on the one who violates the promise.

What is fascinating here is that only Yahweh (represented by the firepot and the flaming torch) passes between these slaughtered animals. In an appearance similar to the theophanies at Sinai in Exodus 3 and 19, Yahweh is the initiator and guarantor of this covenant with Abraham.

> When Abram was ninety-nine years old the Lord appeared to Abram and said to him, 'I am God Almighty; walk before me, and be blameless. And I will make my covenant between me and you, and will multiply you exceedingly.' Then Abram fell on his face; and God said to him, 'Behold, my covenant is with you, and you shall be the father of a multitude of nations. No longer shall your name be Abram, but your name shall be Abraham; for I have made you the father of a multitude of nations. I will make you exceedingly fruitful; and I will make nations of you, and kings shall come forth from you. And I will establish my covenant between me and you

> and your descendants after you throughout their generations
> for an everlasting covenant, to be God to you and to your
> descendants after you. And I will give to you, and to your
> descendents after you, the land of your sojournings, all the
> land of Canaan, for an everlasting possession and I will be
> their God. (Gen 17:1–8)

Up to this point in the Genesis narrative, Abram still has not
seen the realization of Yahweh's promise. Nevertheless, now Yahweh
comes to him again and unilaterally reiterates His covenant. The new
factor in this account is Yahweh's assertion that he will be the God
of Abraham's descendents. Brueggemann suggests that the "formula
clearly presumes the unspoken counter-theme, 'You shall be my people.'"[8] Exodus 6:2–7 offers the full formula:

> And God said to Moses, "I am the Lord. I appeared to
> Abraham, to Isaac, and to Jacob, as God Almighty, but by
> my name 'the Lord' I did not make myself known to them.
> I also established my covenant with them, to give them the
> land of Canaan, the land in which they dwelt as sojourners.
> Moreover I have heard the groaning of the people of Israel
> whom the Egyptians hold in bondage and I have remem-
> bered my covenant. Say therefore to the people of Israel,
> 'I am the Lord, and I will bring you out from under the
> burdens of the Egyptians. And I will deliver you from their
> bondage, and I will redeem you with an outstretched arm
> and with great acts of judgment, and I will take you from my
> people, and I will be your God. . . .'"

God creates a people of promise, a covenant people: "the covenant is the primary metaphor for understanding Israel's life with
God. It is the covenant which offers to Israel the gift of hope, the
reality of identity, the possibility of belonging, the certitude of voca-
tion."[9]

These texts are rich with meaning: they are the fountainhead
of our tradition; yet all we are trying to point out at this time is that
promise, commitment, covenant stand at the heart of Yahweh's way
of dealing with disordered humanity. Covenants are Yahweh's manner
for creating a community of *shalom*. While the words *covenant* and

8 Ibid., 154.
9 Ibid.

vow are not strictly synonymous, they are complementary. Yahweh's covenant with his people expresses some of the same character as the Benedictine vow to brothers or sisters.

2. Yahweh is marked by loyalty and as a practitioner of ḥesed.[10]

O give thanks to the Lord, for he is good, for his loyalty endures forever. (Ps 136:1)[11]

Let us make no mistake; divine loyalty is not merely a supersized version of human loyalty. In much the same way that we humans learn what love is because God taught us by first loving us, we truly learn what loyalty is by understanding the full scope of divine loyalty. It is a given that our own limited versions of love and loyalty will pale in comparison with the love and loyalty of God, but our limits do not remove from us the call to bear witness to this God in our own commitments of love and loyalty.

It may be difficult for twenty-first-century Americans to understand how important God's loyalty was to Israel's faith. Yet, when we consider that, for Yahweh, loyalty and forgiveness are bound together, we can begin to see that it is only by the loyalty of God that such a people as Israel exists. The following formula appears fourteen times in the Old Testament, with slight variations:

But thou art a God ready to forgive, gracious and merciful, slow to anger and abounding in loyalty, and didst not forsake them. (Neh 9:17b)

The faithfulness of God ensures that divine promises will be kept. God's covenant people are totally dependent on the trustworthiness of his promises. We understand that our very existence is dependent on the loyalty of Yahweh. It is little wonder, then, that the language of "faithful loyalty" (and the like) is found in prayers

---

[10] Key studies of *ḥesed* include Glueck, Ḥesed *in the Bible*; Kellenberger, Ḥåsåd wā'åmåt *als ausdruck einer Glaubenserfahrung*; Sakenfeld, *Meaning of* Ḥesed; Sakenfeld, *Faithfulness in Action*. I have long been indebted to Anderson, *Eighth-Century Prophets*. It was Anderson who enlightened my own undergraduate mind to the importance of *ḥesed* for the people of God.

[11] Sakenfeld, *Faithfulness in Action*, 39.

of petition, thanksgiving, and praise. Earthly support may fail, and God's ways may be inscrutable, but the last word, and the first, for Israel is this: "for the LORD is good; his loyalty endures forever, and his faithfulness to all generations" (Ps 100:5).

> He does not retain his anger forever because he delights in loyalty. He will again have compassion upon us, he will tread our iniquities under foot. Thou wilt cast all our sins into the depths of the sea. Thou wilt show faithfulness to Jacob and loyalty to Abraham, as thou hast sworn to our fathers from the days of old. (Mic 7:18–20)

In the end, Yahweh's loyalty overcomes all obstacles. God, whose ways are not like human ways, who is free to let go of Israel and start again, has not and will not let go. Here is the quintessential exercise of loyalty. The One who is forever free chooses to remain bound to this weak and needy people, so that they may bear witness before all peoples that Yahweh alone is God. Of course, this is not an apology for what Bonhoeffer calls "cheap grace." Divine loyalty is never to be confused with cheap grace. God is, indeed, patient and forgiving, but that is not the only word in the biblical witness. Divine loyalty can never be taken for granted even though it is abounding. Past instances of forgiveness provide a ground for hope but never a ground for total assurance that we might continue to live as if Yahweh does not exist. Divine loyalty is extended for a purpose. What is this purpose? It is to reveal to the world the nature of the true God; this is why all forms of idolatry are reprehensible to Yahweh and try his patience above all other missteps. God is patient so that we might be faithful in allowing ourselves to be shaped into his image. God desires a community of *shalom*. God accomplishes this by covenant loyalty (*ḥesed*).

> But the loyalty of the Lord is from everlasting to everlasting upon those who fear him and his righteousness to children's children, to those who keep his covenant and remember to do his commandments. (Ps 103:17–18)

It is a forgotten task of the people of God to bear witness to the loyalty of Yahweh in their own common life. "Israel's core testimony is able to affirm, in the splendor of its faith, that Yahweh's 'steadfast love endures forever.'"[12] While a clear distinction should be upheld between the steadfastness of Yahweh and our own broken attempts at loyalty, one can understand Benedict's vow as a way that the people of God, despite our weakness, might bear a living testimony to Yahweh's loyalty by being loyal to one another.

3. Israel's self-understanding is that it must be a community of promise keeping and fidelity.

> He has showed you, O man, what is good; and what does the Lord require of you but to do justice, and to love loyalty, and to walk humbly with God. (Mic 6:8)

The setting of Micah 6:8 is that of a layperson approaching a cultic official or a priest for information about a proper course of religious action. The inquirer wants to atone for sin by sufficient sacrifice, and the prophet underlines his point by portraying the inquirer going to absurd lengths in suggesting impossible quantities of sacrifice ("thousands of rams rivers of oil") and even a first-born child (Mic 6:6–7). In stark contrast comes the answer: "He has showed you . . . ." What Yahweh requires is justice (*mišpaṭ*), covenant loyalty (*ḥesed*), and trusting humility. I want to focus briefly on the first two requirements.

The call to justice is easily misunderstood. Thanks to our Western tradition, it is difficult to think of justice without assuming that it involves behavior that conforms to an ethical or legal norm. We are used to finding our justice in the courts. When eighth-century prophets such as Micah speak of *mišpaṭ* they are saying something different:

> the eighth century prophets use the terms "justice/righteousness" to refer to the fulfillment of responsibilities that arise out of particular relationships within the community. . . . Each relationship has its specific obligation, and all relationships ultimately are bound by relationship to God. . . . When the demands of various relationships are fulfilled, justice or righteousness prevails and there is *šālôm*, "peace" or "welfare." In short, ethical responsibility is not based on an abstract norm outside of, or above, the relationships of a com-

---

[12] Brueggemann, *Theology of the Old Testament*, 313.

munity, but is motivated by the demands and blessings of
life in community, within which persons are bound together
in various relations and in relation with God.[13]

Above all, it was clear that Yahweh's *ḥesed* was expressed through
covenantal loyalty and steadfast love. What might it look like for
Yahweh's people to practice *ḥesed*? Certainly it means that we must
fulfill our covenantal obligations toward Yahweh, but this obligation
must be made "manifest in the faithful performance of responsibilities that strengthen and maintain the community. Yahweh has shown
them 'what is good' through his 'saving acts' that demonstrate his
spontaneous love and sensitive concern, but the people have failed to
imitate his salutary actions."[14]

In the Gospel of Matthew, Jesus twice instructs us to go and
learn what this means: "I desire mercy and not sacrifice" (Matt 9:10–
13; 12:1–8). Jesus is quoting Hosea 6:6:

> For I desire loyalty, not [animal] sacrifice,
> the knowledge of God, not whole burnt offerings."[15]

This passage in Hosea is part of a larger literary unit that begins
in 5:8 and extends as far as 7:16.[16] Israel is in crisis and attempts to
address the crisis by returning to religion, but a return to religion
does not necessarily mean a return to God. The difference is stated
clearly in Hosea 6:6. Yahweh has no concern for the sacrificial cult;
he desires *ḥesed*. The Greek rendering of *ḥesed* in Matthew's Gospel
as *elios* is unfortunate. *Ḥesed* certainly involves mercy, but such a
translation loses what it is that Yahweh is truly after. "The loyalty
which God desires involves freely chosen follow-through on commitment. No doubt it refers at one level to a style of life in community which is lacking in Israel. But context suggests that here loyalty
is directed toward God as well as toward other people."[17] Yahweh's is
not a call to elaborate worship services but a call to know him and
worship him with *ḥesed* and *mišpaṭ*.

---

[13] Anderson, *Eighth-Century Prophets*, 43.

[14] Ibid., 49–50.

[15] Anderson's translation; see ibid., 54.

[16] Wolff, *Hosea*, 103–30.

[17] Sakenfeld, *Faithfulness in Action*, 106–7.

Yahweh's people are called to imitation. We are called to be holy, not according to our own standards of holiness—but as he is holy. This is what it means to walk humbly with Yahweh. Trusting his vision for human community, we give ourselves to the practices of *mišpaṭ* and *ḥesed* as practiced by our God. The justice and loyalty expected is clearly directed toward the coming-into-being of a shalom community.

Only tentative conclusions can be drawn with regard to the ecclesial practice of making vows. All that can be confidently said is that Yahweh is a covenant-making God, that Yahweh practices *ḥesed*, that his steadfast love endures forever, and that Yahweh also expects his covenant people to be characterized by *ḥesed* and *mišpaṭ* (and certainly by humility as well). When seen through this paradigm, Benedict's vow making seems to be a step attempting authentic faithfulness to who Yahweh is and to what his intentions are for humanity.

NEW TESTAMENT CONSIDERATIONS

Righteousness (*dikaiosynē*) and love (*agapē*) are the words of the New Testament (particularly for Paul) that function much the same way that *mišpaṭ* and *ḥesed* function in the Old Testament. I am not trying to make a linguistic claim here but rather a theological one.

Righteousness

Any understanding of what it might mean for the people of God to be righteous must begin with the nature of God's righteousness. What characterizes the righteousness of God? How is it that God is righteous? The New Testament speaks of the "righteousness of God," but the meaning of this phrase is somewhat disputed. Shaped by Reformation debates, some Protestant traditions hold that the phrase "the righteousness of God" refers to an imputed status that believers receive. Hence, when Paul states that in the gospel "the righteousness of God is revealed through faith for faith" (Rom 1:17), we are to assume that believers receive a righteousness of their own, imputed to them by God in response to their faith.

In contrast to this classic Reformation position, it seems clear that Paul uses the phrase "the righteousness of God" to refer to God's own righteousness as a quality that God possesses. The quality in question is clearly God's faithfulness to his promises, to his covenant. "God's righteousness" is a quality in action, meaning that when we speak of the "righteousness of God," we are not merely talking about an attribute of God but are also talking about actions of God: actions that embody God's covenant faithfulness.[18]

So, what is the character of the righteousness of God? According to Paul, when we speak of the righteousness of God, we speak of God's covenant faithfulness. This is both a quality in God and an active power that goes out in expression of that faithfulness.

> But now, apart from law, the righteousness of God has been disclosed, and is attested by the law and the prophets, the righteousness of God through faith in Jesus Christ for all who believe. For there is no distinction, since all have sinned and fall short of the glory of God; they are now justified by his grace as a gift, through the redemption that is in Christ Jesus, whom God put forward as a sacrifice of atonement by his blood, effective through faith. He did this to show his righteousness, because in his divine forbearance he had passed over the sins previously committed; it was to prove at the present time that he himself is righteous and that he justifies the one who has faith in Jesus. (Rom 3:21–26)

The law and the prophets attest to the righteousness of God. But God's righteousness has been most fully disclosed in Jesus Christ, who is God's justifying gift and the expression of God's own righteousness. The blood and sacrifice language is covenantal language and serves to underscore that Jesus is God's honoring of his covenant with Israel. In Christ, God has made good as the guarantor of the covenant and has been true to his covenant promises, bringing blessing upon the nations, taking the weight of their alienating sin upon himself. God reconciled humanity to himself, so that nothing would stand in the way of a renewal of covenant partnership. In reconciling humanity, God has revealed his righteousness by exercising "divine forbearance."

God expresses God's own righteousness by being faithful to his promises, by "sticking it out" with sinful humanity, by sacrificing himself for the sake of the redemption of humanity. Hence, if we are

---

[18] An excellent yet accessible introduction to this argument is Wright, "Justification and the Church," 113–34.

going to speak in broad strokes about the content of righteousness as revealed in the agency of God, we must speak in ways that reflect on the life of Jesus, and we must speak in a fashion that uses the language of relational faithfulness, promise keeping, patience, and self-sacrifice.

When the New Testament speaks of the righteousness of God, it sounds very similar to the ways in which the Old Testament speaks of Yahweh: as a God who is a loyal covenant maker and keeper for the sake of creation.[19]

For Paul it is clear that God's righteous activity was for the sake of humanity, so that humanity might exhibit similar life-giving activity. In 2 Corinthians 5, Paul asserts that Jesus died for all, so that we might no longer live for ourselves but for him who died and was raised for us. In light of this act of God, we no longer view anyone from a human point of view, but from a "righteousness-of-God" point of view, because we have been given the same ministry of reconciliation:

> So we are ambassadors for Christ, since God is making his appeal through us; we entreat you on behalf of Christ, be reconciled to God. For our sake he made him to be sin who knew no sin, so that in him we might become the righteousness of God. (2 Cor 5:20–21)

Some commentators on 2 Corinthians 5 seem to imply that the capacity to be ambassadors for Christ is a function of the apostolic office. Against this it must be asserted that "we" is not exclusively an apostolic "we." If the "we" were purely an apostolic "we," then the idea of "ambassador" (and the following "righteousness of God") would be exclusively associated with the apostolic office. Paul and Timothy, though, come exhorting the Corinthians to share in their ministry of reconciliation, a ministry that would include the Corinthians' also becoming ambassadors for Christ. It seems self-evident that the "we" of vv. 20–21 is inclusive rather than oriented

---

[19] An entire additional study could be given over to the relationship between God's *mišpaṭ* and his righteousness and/or justice. Suffice it to say, for the moment, that both testaments assume a *telos* of *shalom* regardless of the term being used leading to a great similarity of meaning for these words. Western concepts of justice have perverted our English readings of these texts and are in great need of correction in our churches.

toward some exclusive concept such as office. Otherwise, the passage would read as follows: "So, we apostles are ambassadors for Christ, since God is making his appeal through the apostolic office, we entreat you on behalf of Christ, be reconciled to God. For the sake of us apostles, he made him to be sin who knew no sin, so that in him, we apostles might become the righteousness of God."

A reading of 2 Corinthians 5 that restricts the ministry of reconciliation to apostles is untenable. First, such a reading would be problematic in that it would take the teeth out of Paul's exhortation to the Corinthian congregation. Second, such a reading is inconsistent with Paul's ecclesiology in 2 Corinthians, a book in which we find no such emphasis on office. Third, a restricted reading of 2 Corinthians 5:20–21 would exclude the Pauline concept of "imitation" (see 1 Cor 4:16; Phil 3:17; and 2 Thess 3:7–9).

Paul understands that he and Timothy are ambassadors appealing to their brothers and sisters in Corinth to share in the ministry of reconciliation. God's reconciling work in Christ was done so that all who believe might become the righteousness of God. Simply put, Paul's hope is that the Corinthians will join Timothy and himself in the ministry of reconciliation. To do so, the Corinthians must exhibit a life, both in one another's presence as individuals and collectively together, that witnesses to the righteousness of God. Such a witness would entail a common life that displays the characteristics of relational faithfulness, patience, and self-sacrifice. Paul's hope is that the Corinthians' own faith might take on qualities of faithfulness to one another, of sticking it out together in spite of sinfulness, and of sacrificial living, so that others might experience the life-giving power of the gospel. When the Corinthians order their common life in such a fashion, they themselves are ambassadors for Christ.

When a community enters into a vow such as the threefold promise of the Benedictines, it is in fact bearing witness to the ways and means by which God has chosen to engage humanity. A community of promise acts as an ambassador for Christ, testifying to God's faithfulness, patience, and trustworthiness. In light of such enacted testimony of God's faithfulness, it is not difficult to see how Benedict's vow or a similar commitment might be a righteous way for the people of God to be faithful to their calling.

Agapē

Our definition of *agapē* comes from the character and action of God.

> Beloved, let us love one another, because love is from God; everyone who loves is born of God and knows God. Whoever does not love does not know God, for God is love. God's love was revealed among us in this way: God sent his only Son into the world so that we might live through him. In this is love, not that we loved God but that he loved us and sent his Son to be the atoning sacrifice for our sins. Beloved, since God loved us so much, we also ought to love one another. (1 John 4:7–11)

> We know love by this, that he laid down his life for us—and we ought to lay down our lives for one another. (1 John 3:16)

Knowledge of *agapē* begins with knowing God and knowing the nature of God's *agapē* toward us. As we saw above with righteousness (and showing great similarity to *ḥesed* and *mišpaṭ*), God's *agapē* is bound up with his covenantal faithfulness—most fully expressed in the atoning self-giving of Jesus. The common themes of God's relational faithfulness, promise keeping, patience, and self-sacrifice are apparent in any consideration of the nature of God's *agapē*. Paul makes clear that our own understanding of *agapē* entails similar commitments.

> If I speak in the tongues of mortals and of angels, but do not have love, I am a noisy gong or a clanging symbol. And if I have prophetic powers, and understand all mysteries and all knowledge, and if I have all faith, so as to remove mountains, but do not have love, I am nothing. If I give away all my possessions, and if I hand over my body so that I may boast, but do not have love, I gain nothing. Love is patient; love is kind; love is not envious or boastful or arrogant or rude. It does not insist on its own way; it is not irritable or resentful; it does not rejoice in wrongdoing, but rejoices in the truth. It bears all things, believes all things, hopes all things, endures all things. Love never ends. But as for prophecies, they will come to an end; as for tongues, they will cease; as for knowledge, it will come to an end. For we

know only in part, and we prophesy only in part; but when the complete comes, the partial will come to an end. When I was a child, I spoke like a child, I thought like a child, I reasoned like a child; when I became an adult, I put an end to childish ways. For now we see in a mirror, dimly, but then we will see face to face. Now I know only in part; then I will know fully, even as I have been fully known. And now faith, hope, and love abide, these three; and the greatest of these is love. (1 Cor 13:1–13).

Some would see chapter 13 as an interruption of the discussion about spiritual gifts. Jean Héring is quite clear in this respect, claiming that the idea in chapter 13 is that *agapē* is to be placed above the charismatic gifts valued so highly by some Corinthians, but that chapter 13 is "quite unrelated to Chapters 12 and 14."[20] On the other hand Grosheide argues that chapter 13 is not an interruption but is "a necessary link in the argument which has its purpose to assign glossolalia its rightful place."[21] Others see chapter 13 as characteristic of rhetoric oriented to a public presentation.[22] Regardless, it appears to clearly be the case that Paul is using chapter 13 to reinforce his argument for the unity of the body in Corinth. The language is almost poetic and Paul certainly draws from the rhetorical traditions to make his point. If chapter 13 is a rhetorical digression, it is not a digression away from Paul's appeal for unity, but a digression in order to underline the point that Paul is making: We really need one another, because the work of the Church lives on *agapē*. Without *agapē*, the other gifts are fruitless. Tongues, prophecy, understanding of the mysteries, gnosis, even faith, sacrifice/generosity, and the handing over of our bodies are nothing without *agapē*. Specifically, Corinth will live or die by its response to *agapē*. Witherington notes, "John Chrysostom saw each clause of 1 Cor. 13:4–7 as an antidote for the sickness of Corinthian factionalism (*Hom.* 34.1, *NPNF* 1 XII, 201f.)."[23]

The language of 1 Corinthians 13 is familiar to Christian and non-Christian alike; especially well known are vv. 4–7. These verses

[20] Héring. *First Epistle*, 134.
[21] Grosheide, *Commentary*, 303.
[22] Witherington, *Conflict*, 264–65.
[23] Ibid., 265.

have become a common language in our culture, used in many a marriage ceremony—secular and religious. The language abounds in various greeting cards and in popular literature. So much so that for many, the language has become trite and sentimental, often devoid of its original power of meaning. Richard Hays comments with his usual clarity: "Paul's lyrical prose in this unit has encouraged many readers to take it out of context as a lovely meditation of the nature of love. . . ."[24] Hays rejects such a perspective, understanding that rather than functioning as a digression or insertion, chapter 13 actually serves to help the reader understand 12 and 14 better. When we read this section as a meditation on the nature of love, abstracted from its context, we are too free to interject our own definition of "love" into the "lyric." Our culture is just as apt to think that eros is patient as it is to dig deep into understanding the nature of *agapē*. So, what can we say about *agapē* from a reading of 1 Corinthians 13:4–7? We have two different ways of summarizing—the negative way and the positive way. Compare these two lists:

The negative (what *agapē* isn't):
- short-tempered
- intolerant of any suffering
- cold
- unkind
- jealous
- envious
- a braggart
- a show-off
- puts oneself forward
- inflated sense of one's own importance
- arrogant
- egocentric at the expense of courtesy
- dishonorable
- shameful
- preoccupied with the interests of self
- hot-tempered
- irritable
- easily provoked or exasperated

[24] Hays. *First Corinthians*, 221.

- plays the accountant with regard to the wrongs of others
- happy to see others brought down a notch
- fears the truth
- hates to rejoice when truth embraces "the other"
- refuses to support
- refuses to protect or bear up all
- refuses to believe the best about "the other"
- tires of support
- loses faith
- exhausts hope
- gives up
- refuses to put up with "the other,"
- falls
- fails
- self-centered

The positive (what *agapē* is):

- patient
- long-suffering
- kind
- open
- generous
- hospitable
- tolerant
- trusting
- understanding
- humble
- self-deprecating
- realistic sense of self
- looks to put others forward
- courteous, honorable
- preoccupied with the good of others
- even-tempered
- amiable
- obliging
- gracious
- easygoing
- believes the best of others

- quick to forgive and quick to forget
- wants the best for others
- hopes for mercy for others
- celebrates occasions of grace
- loves the truth
- open
- vulnerable
- supports steadfastly
- faithful
- hopeful
- enduring
- runs the race to the end
- grows in strength as time moves on
- other-centered

Agapē is by its very nature other-centered. What *agapē* is not is self-centered.[25] With regard to spiritual gifts, *agapē* qualifies as the greatest spiritual gift. Prophecy, tongues, service, gnosis, even faith, are all subject to abusive self-interest. Other forms of love may also fall captive to self-interest; without *agapē*, they are nothing. Yet *agapē*, by definition, cannot be self-centered, for it is love that is turned away from the self and toward the other.

It appears clear that God, as revealed to Paul in Christ Jesus, is the one who gives definition to Paul's idea of *agapē*. Anthony Thiselton, in his excellent commentary on 1 Corinthians states it like this:

> First, **love** represents "the power of the new age" breaking into the present, "the only vital force which has a future." **Love** is that quality which distinctively stamps the life of heaven, where regard and respect for the other dominates the character of life with God as the communion of saints and heavenly hosts. . . . Second, . . . **love** denotes above all a *stance* or *attitude* which shows itself *in acts of will* as

[25] When I make this claim for the other-centered nature of *agapē*, I am not making a claim that *agapē* is disinterested love. I presume that in order for the "other" to exist, there must be an accompanying self. Hence, other-centered love is not disinterested, it does realize the delightful and joyful communion that the best other-centered loving can bring mutually to all selves engaged in communion initiated by the move from self-centeredness to other-centeredness.

regard, respect, and concern for the welfare of the other. It is therefore profoundly *christological*, for *the cross* is the paradigm case of the act of *will* and *stance* which *places welfare of others above the interests of the self.* Here Moltmann and Jüngel rightly relate this to the *self-giving grace of the cruciform, Christomorphic God.*[26]

It is difficult not to get distracted by the relevance and importance of *agapē* for the life of Christian community and to prattle on when the only point that is trying to be made here is that there are some substantial theological connection points between the New Testament idea of *agapē* and the Old Testament expressions of *ḥesed* and *mišpaṭ*. The New Testament does present a vision of God and of the people of God that exhibits continuity with the Old Testament witness. God desires the formation of a people who practice *ḥesed*, *mišpaṭ*, and *agapē* (and it should be apparent by now that these are fluid, overlapping concepts.). The language of covenant faithfulness, steadfast love, self-sacrifice, patience, long-suffering, vulnerable, enduring, loyalty, and promise appears to justify vow making as an appropriate expression for the people of God.

Conclusion

Despite my social location as a free-church American from the western United States, I can find no merit to the argument that vow making is mere "popishness" or pharisaical legalism. If we are going to take seriously the ways that God interacts with creation, and if we are going to make any attempt to mimic God's interaction as our politic (or church order), then we are going to have to conclude that the making of vows is a legitimate, if not an essential, Christian practice. We might even call the practice of vow making prophetic, in that vow making will often prove to tell the truth to the world around us, and in that vow making will never fail to tell the truth to us who enter into vows. Our vows will always expose us to both the tragedies and joys that are the bane and the blessing of our humanity. Communities who live by vows may not always function as cities set on a hill, but, if they will be honest with themselves, they will always be confronted with the truth of who they are.

[26] Thiselton, *First Epistle*, 1035.

Conversion

Jonathan Wilson-Hartgrove

When Jesus shows up in the gospels, he has an announcement to make—a declaration that begins with a command: "Repent," Jesus says, "for the kingdom of God is at hand." Repentance, which is the beginning of conversion, is also the beginning of the gospel. The good news that another reality is breaking into the world demands a fundamental transformation of all who hear it. To be part of this new world order—this "new humanity" as Paul will name it—we have to die to ourselves and get "born again" as members of Christ's body. This is necessary because Jesus *is* the gospel that he has come to proclaim. Said differently, the medium is the message. Jesus himself is our call to conversion.

But the word *conversion* has been co-opted in the modern world by a culture obsessed with individualism and bent on making religion a matter of personal piety. So we organize events called "crusades" (or, more recently, "festivals"), call people to "ask Jesus into their hearts," and count conversions by the number of those who make "first-time professions of faith." Unfortunately, we who have learned to profess Christianity in this way appear no more like Christ in actual practice than anyone else in America. Despite all our talk about holiness, evangelicals are pretty much like everyone else when it comes to divorce rates, premarital sex, domestic abuse, and use of pornography. When you look at the numbers, we don't stand out as a people "set apart"—except that we're *more likely* to be racist. And the more money we have, the less likely we are to share it with the poor.[1] Maybe the most disturbing trend is that our churches do not,

---

[1] For a more thorough analysis of these contradictions within evangelicalism, see Sider, *Scandal.* To be fair to evangelicals (I am one, after all), I should also note Christian Smith's work, which demonstrates both the diversity and the complexity of evangelical thought and practice on most any topic. The moral majority is not, in fact, an overwhelming majority anymore. We're a varied bunch. See especially Smith, *American Evangelicalism;* and Smith, *Christian America?*

by and large, recognize this miserliness as a glaring condemnation of American Christianity. Without belittling the importance of professing Christ as Lord or denying the significance of conversion experiences, this chapter assumes that Christians in twenty-first-century America are in desperate need of new spaces where the experience of a personal relationship with Jesus is not privatized but rather made public and active in the life of a community. What we most need are schools for conversion.

Conversatio morum is one part of the threefold vow that St. Benedict prescribes for adherents to his rule. It is often translated "conversion of life," though Anthony Meisel and M. L. del Mastro render it simply "to live as a monk" (RB 58:17).[2] Conversion is, in the most basic of terms, the gift of a new way to live. It is, in Benedict's wisdom, to know the joy of Christ in the work of one's daily life by taking up the "all powerful and righteous arms of obedience to fight under the true King, the Lord Jesus Christ" (RB P:3). Thus the triviality of our transitory existence is transformed into an epic adventure of cosmic proportions in which we contend on God's side. Conversion means the whole world is changed. "If anyone is in Christ Jesus, behold—new creation!" (2 Cor 5:17). To be converted is to live in a whole new world.

Two Sides of Conversion

If we follow Benedict in a study of Scripture for the sake of conversion, two complementary dynamics of conversion emerge. They might best be summarized in a brief look at the original Greek and Hebrew words for *conversion*, though we must see that this is not a division between the testaments. It is not as if the first dynamic is revealed in the Old Testament and the second in the New. No, both are there all along. I do not distinguish between the two dynamics in order to separate them. My point is just the opposite: I want to make a distinction that I hope clarifies the true nature of conversion—that it is always the combination of two dynamics. Like light. In high school physics class, I learned that light is both a wave and a particle. This is a distinction my teacher made to help me understand the

---

[2] Unless otherwise noted, all quotations from Benedict's Rule come from Meisel and del Maestro, *Rule of St. Benedict.*

complexity of light. The point was not that I could ever separate the two dynamics. Light is always both at the same time. But I would understand light better if I knew that it is both a wave and a particle. The same is true of the two dynamics of conversion. You can never have one without the other. But understanding each dynamic helps us see the true nature (and wonder!) of conversion among the people of God.

The Greek word *metanoia*, which we have already seen translated as "repent" in Jesus's announcement of his kingdom, is literally a "change of mind." It is the joining together of *meta*, as in *metamorphosis* and *noia*, as in *noetic*. But it is important to note that the Greek for "mind" (*nous*) is just as often translated "heart." So we could also say *metanoia* is a "change of heart and mind," where heart is not just a center of emotion, and mind is not just the locus of thought, but where both are shorthand for the soul—the inner essence of God's human creatures. This is what Paul calls the "inner man" in King James English. The soul is the part of us that we have the hardest time knowing in a world of almost infinite external stimuli and advertisements, all designed to create desires we didn't have before. Conversion is about a transformation of our inner life, where will and thought and feeling intersect. *Metanoia* means the renewal of ourselves from the inside out. This is the first dynamic of conversion.

But there is at the same time a second dynamic. In Hebrew, repentance is signified by variations of the root word *shuv*, which means "to turn" or "to return." It is a physical word, involving bodily movement, especially movement of the feet. To turn toward God is to set one's feet on a new path, forsaking the road that leads to destruction to walk in the way that leads to life. *Shuv* is the people of Israel returning from exile in Babylon to be God's holy people in the Promised Land. Conversion has a form, then. It means becoming part of a people. And not just any people. Conversion means adoption into the chosen people of God. "The LORD your God has chosen you to be a people for His own possession out of all the peoples who are on the face of the earth" (Deut 7:6). To his chosen people God gave the gift of a law. That law is a description of what life together with God looks like. As with any law, it is a basis for life in community—what we usually call *political* life. So conversion is political. Turning to God is not only about the inner condition of our souls; it also has to do with the external form of our life together in community. Conversion is a way of life that must be practiced.

In an essay on St. Benedict's vow of *conversio morum*, Macrina Sitzia points to both the interior and the exterior dynamics of conversion in the Rule. "It might seem," she writes, "that we have indicated two distinct and separate means of initiation: the ritual or liturgical, and what might easily be termed the psychological, that is, an interior process. For St. Benedict the point is that the two should become one."[3] American Christianity could certainly learn from Benedict's wisdom. In a context where evangelicals stress a "conversion experience" and Catholics practice catechesis, the grassroots ecumenism of a new monasticism offers the hope of schools for conversion in which the modern divisions between inner and outer, private and public, cease to exist because both dynamics of conversion are integrated in the daily life of communities.

This essay seeks to show that each dynamic of conversion is rooted in Scripture and that both work together in the Bible's greatest models of life with God. I pray that the same Spirit who stirred the waters at creation and moved the writers of Holy Scripture will compel the hearts of Christians in America to seek authentic conversion in community. I can testify that the Spirit has, at least, so moved me. I am learning that to live is to turn (and return) to God together with my wife, Leah, and other friends at Rutba House, a community of new monasticism in the Walltown neighborhood of Durham, North Carolina. It is a gift both to be in the process of conversion and to write about it here. What I have to say in this chapter is inevitably dependent on our life together at Rutba House.

As Benedict says, "Let us encompass ourselves with faith and the practice of good works, and guided by the Gospel, tread the path He has cleared for us. Thus may we deserve to see Him, who has called us into his kingdom" (RB P:21). I invite you to do the same. Read on in prayer. And if in the course of reading you have the opportunity to serve Christ in your neighbor (as I just did while writing), then, by all means, lay this book aside. Conversion is about learning to welcome God into our lives.

[3] Sitzia, "Benedictine Vow," 232.

John says in his first epistle that "when we see [Christ], we will be like him" (1 John 3:2), which is, no doubt, the true end of conversion. Our minds are changed so that we might have the mind of Christ. Our bodies are turned toward God so we might become members of his living body. In Jesus, our conversion is complete. With him, new life is always now.

I. Contemplation and Conversion: The Inward Turn

In the middle of a carefully constructed argument about what it means for Christians to have the mind of Christ, Paul asks the Corinthians, "What human being knows what is truly human except the human spirit that is within?" (1 Cor 2:11). This is a funny question to our modern ears. Paul clearly expects his reader to answer, "No one." No one knows what is truly human except by the spirit that is within. This was the common wisdom of the world in which Scripture was written. From this premise, Paul wants to argue by analogy that just as the Corinthians know what is true about them by their spirits, so, too, the only way to know God is by God's Spirit. That is the point of this quotation about the "human spirit that is within." Paul's claim is not exactly a claim of Scripture. Paul doesn't seem to think any special revelation is required to say that the true life is the inner life. Paul simply appeals to the common sense of the biblical world. Everyone knows that the true life is the inner life. To know what is truly human one must know the human spirit that is within.

But we in the modern world don't share in common this sense of the inner spirit. We were told by the empiricists that what could not be seen was not real. The existence of an inner life was not reasonable because it was not scientifically verifiable. Yet we could not deny the stirrings within us. So psychology taught us to see and name our inner experiences. Rather, it taught us that someone else (i.e. an expert) could see and name them—and, perhaps, manipulate them—for a price. Thus, we created a "therapeutic culture" in which our psyches—that is, our spirits—are the potentially volatile part of our selves that must be controlled. Controlled not by some god, but by us. By Society. The psyche that will not bow to public opinion shall be called deviant.

Deviance has come in a variety of forms, many of which may be characterized generally as a turn to the East. A great majority of spirits in the West who have rebelled against this psychologizing of the inner life have turned to Eastern religions and to their contemplative practices. There these seekers have found once again the common wisdom that Paul assumed—that to know what is truly human one must know the human spirit within. They have learned it from Zen masters and from Sufi poetry; from Gandhi and from Thich Nhat Hanh. The many sources agree because this is human wisdom. It is what humans know by looking within themselves.

The inward turn, however, has proved difficult for heirs of the modern world. Even those of us who see the need to learn from the East struggle to put the wisdom into practice. What could it possibly mean to be a contemplative in New York City? How would you survive? Who might your friends be? The wisdom of the East, though it rings true, seems so impractical that it has been idealized or disregarded as radically sectarian. Spirituality in America is a leisure activity that gets a shelf in the bookstore beside Fiction and Fantasy. There is, no doubt, a market for it. But that is just the problem; to the extent the inner life is commodified for consumption by autonomous individuals, its wisdom has already been ignored. The point of inner wisdom is that it is of infinite value. It "knows what is truly human," Paul says. To reduce such a gift to a product is to reject it.

But even if the gift of inner wisdom is accepted, the human problem of sin is not solved. For the modern world is not our only problem. The modern world is merely the particular context of broken creation that we find ourselves in right now. Though the existence of an inner life was something Paul could assume, he had more to say to the Corinthians. Paul wasn't just passing on common wisdom. He thought he had real news to proclaim: "No one comprehends what is truly God's except the Spirit of God. Now we have received not the spirit of the world, but the Spirit that is from God, so that we may understand the gifts bestowed on us by God" (1 Cor 2:11–12). Paul is excited because he thinks he received a special gift—a gift from the Creator of the universe. While most anyone in first-century Corinth would have known about an inner life of the spirit, peculiar for the Corinthian Christians to believe was that they had unique access to the maker of heaven and earth. But Paul insisted that they did. As a matter of fact, he maintained that this was their *only* claim on God—that they had been given God's Spirit. And that's not all.

God's Holy Spirit was supposed to teach them how to understand *all* the gifts God had given them—their human spirits included.

Not all inner lives are created equal, then. While a turn to the spiritual may be a turn away from Western culture, it is not necessarily a turn towards the God who is revealed in Jesus Christ. Only from God's Spirit do we learn how to receive the gift of a spirit. But God's Spirit, Paul claims, has already given us a gift unimaginable: "We have the mind of Christ," he declares (1 Cor 2:16). We who have been baptized into Christ's body, into the church, have received the mind of the second person of the Trinity. Our inner lives are now located in the inner life of God. At the center of our being is not an autonomous self, but rather the three-personed God "in whom we live and move and have our very being" (Acts 17:28).

So contemplation is not narcissism—is not a turn in on one's self, because we have been and are being converted. We have the mind of Christ and are being changed within to be the sort of people who can say with Jesus, "I have come . . . not to do my own will but the will of him who sent me" (John 6:38). My will, which I used to call my true self, is being replaced by the will of God. Or, more precisely, inner conversion means that my false self is dying so that my true self can be raised to eternal life. Conversion is always about becoming who I really am—a creature created in God's image. The "mind of Christ" is Paul's word picture for the shape of inner conversion, of what God's image looks like when pressed into the human spirit. In order to see what we shall be, we have to learn how to think the thoughts and to feel the passion of Jesus. Which is to say, again, we look within to look to God. Only as we inhabit the mind of Christ do we learn to see what conversion looks like.

Inhabiting the Mind of Christ

In his letter to the Philippians, Paul describes the landscape of Christ's mind by singing a praise hymn. "Let the same mind be in you that was in Christ Jesus," he begins.

> Who though he was in the form of God,
> did not regard equality with God
> as something to be exploited,
> but emptied himself,

> taking the form of a slave,
> being born in human likeness.
> And being found in human form,
> he humbled himself
> and became obedient to the point of death—
> even death on a cross.
>
> Therefore God also highly exalted him
> and gave him the name
> that is above every name,
> so that at the name of Jesus
> every knee should bend,
> in heaven and on earth and under the earth,
> and every tongue confess
> that Jesus Christ is Lord,
> to the glory of God the Father. (Phil 2:5–11)

Paul unveils the inner life of Christ by describing Jesus' outward action in light of his divine nature. Because Paul understands that Jesus Christ was "in the form of God" by his very nature, he is able to see into Christ's spirit and to assert that Jesus "did not regard equality with God as something to be exploited." Because he knows who Jesus is, Paul sees Christ's inner self played out in the drama of his life. That God's Son took on human flesh in Jesus shows us great humility. That Jesus was a servant and not a master demonstrates the self-giving nature of his spirit. That he died on a cross despite his wish that the suffering be removed is a testimony to his obedience. So in one short stanza, we learn that humility, self-giving love, and obedience mark the mind in which we are to find our true selves. To be who I really am in Christ, I will have to learn to think humbly, to feel compassion, to want obedience. My first response must always be to confess that these thoughts, feelings, and desires are not my inner life most of the time. I begin to inhabit the mind of Christ by naming as sin this lack of humility, compassion, and obedience. Conversion of the heart and mind is dependent upon the practice of confession.

Every day at Rutba House, we say together a simple prayer of confession as part of our evening prayers. In a newsletter article entitled "Praying is Believing," Tim Otto wrote,

> I'm so glad that our routine includes a confession of our sinfulness. Coming to Rutba, I worried that once people knew my sinfulness that it would be clear that I didn't belong. But we all signed up to be Christians because we were, and are, sinners. That prayer helps us remember that, and helps us not become Pharisees.[4]

So confessing our lack of humility, among other sins, we are humbled. Despite our deep brokenness—indeed, *because* of its exposure to the light of God's grace—we have the mind of Christ. Little by little, we learn to humble ourselves.

For me, nothing is more humiliating than the time of personal sharing that comes at the end of our week together. It is part of our weekly house meeting on Sunday evenings at Rutba House. We call it "checking in." Each of us has ten to fifteen minutes to review our week out loud in front of brothers and sisters, who know us well. I am most often embarrassed by how little insight I have into my own inner life and the significance of the week's events. My embarrassment, of course, is due to my own pride—my desire to appear more spiritually mature and self-aware than I really am. And so I am confronted once again with the depth of my sinfulness.

But confession isn't just about how I understand what's going on inside me. The trouble with sin is that it twists my thoughts and feelings. It makes it hard for me to see the ways I'm fooling myself, even in confession. "The heart is deceitful above all things and beyond cure," Jeremiah says. "Who can understand it?" (Jer 17:9). I know I can't. But in community, God has given me others to help me name my sin. Because others have to live with me, they have some interest in helping me grow up in Christ. And because they've promised to stick it out with me in love, I can trust them enough to listen—at least, that's my promise to them. Part of my growing up is learning to be a better listener.

Weekly check-ins help me to name the particulars of my sin. They make my daily confession concrete. As I repeat with the same

[4] Otto, "Praying is Believing."

eight people every evening, "we confess that we have sinned against you in thought, word, and deed, by what we have done and by what we have left undone," I understand more each time what we are saying. Understanding it, I feel it. I feel the ways my sin separates me from these people whom I so want to love. I feel the pain that others have shared with me, as I watch them struggle with their own sin. But I also feel the grace of each one of them bearing with me in my sin. I feel compassion when I had felt anger sometimes only minutes before. I understand the mercy of God in the simple fact that we keep going, remaining committed to each other, even as we know one another well enough to say just how each of us is twisted by sin. I am often comforted by words from a letter that Clarence Jordan, founder of Koinonia Farms, wrote to his son after decades of life in a neomonastic community: "This is what always baffles me," he wrote. "Koinonia is forever dying and forever living. We should have conked out long ago, but somehow others came in the nick of time. This half-born condition is agonizing, and I could wish it otherwise, but there it is."[5]

The Psalter as School of Prayer

In this "half-born condition" we find ourselves in, we are always in the midst of turning, always being converted even as we cling to the promise that we already have the mind of Christ. The humility, compassion, and obedience that we see in Jesus and know to be the thoughts and feelings of our true selves are nevertheless habits of the heart and mind that we must learn. Confession is a constant reminder that our spirits need a school for conversion. For St. Benedict and those who have followed his rule over the past 1500 years, the Psalter has been such a school for the conversion of their spirits. Learning to pray the psalms is also one of the principal tasks we have committed our spirits to at Rutba House.

St. Benedict said that the brothers in his monastery should not be overly burdened by a commitment to pray the whole Psalter every week because the Fathers of the church had prayed the Psalter every day! (RB 18:25) With the help of electric lighting and the time-saving aids of modern technology (I use an electric beard trimmer, among

---

[5] Clarence Jordan to his son, February 27, 1966, quoted in Marsh, *Beloved Community*, 84.

other gadgets), we manage to pray one psalm in the morning and a second in the evening each weekday at Rutba House. That means, given our days off (we don't gather for corporate prayer on the weekends), we pray the whole Psalter through just under six times a year. And, even at that, we sometimes grow weary. (I particularly grow weary of Psalm 119, a portion of which is assigned every Wednesday in the daily lectionary from the *Book of Common Prayer,* which we use.) So, if the Psalter is a school for prayer, then it would be fair to say that I am the equivalent of a kindergartener. Nevertheless, I am grateful for what I have learned and am learning.

Because the Psalter is Holy Scripture, which we believe to be the Word of God, learning to pray the psalms is something like learning to speak to God in God's own language. Or, at least, it is learning to speak God's Word for us back to God. Just as all creation was made from nothing by the Word of God, so, too, are our hearts and minds remade as we learn to think, feel, and desire with God by learning the prayers of the Psalter. Once again, the Spirit that inspired Scripture is speaking to reveal to us the inner life of God. Praying the words of Scripture, our spirits are transformed.

But you don't have to pray the psalms very long to realize that they are not only the Word of God but also the words of people. They are words already directed toward God from a wide variety of human situations. Sometimes they are angry, as in Psalm 137: "Happy shall they be who pay you back what you have done to us! Happy shall they be who take your little ones and dash them against the rock!" (vv. 8–9) Sometimes they are weighed down with guilt, as in Psalm 51: "Have mercy on me, O God, according to your steadfast love; according to your abundant mercy blot out my transgressions. Wash me thoroughly from my iniquity, and cleanse me from my sin" (vv.1–2). Sometimes they are exultant, as in Psalm 150: "Let everything that has breath praise the Lord! Praise the Lord!" (v. 6). Sometimes they are the words of a desperate beggar, as in Psalm 40: "Be pleased, O Lord, to deliver me; O Lord, make haste to help me. . . . As for me, I am poor and needy, but the Lord takes thought for me. You are my help and my deliverer; do not delay, O my God" (vv. 13, 17). Always they are deeply human words, spoken from the heights and depths of reality. The Psalms cover the range of human thought and emotion. In them we discover the spirit of God's chosen people.

Historically, the Psalter is the collected prayer of the people called Israel. Just where all the prayers came from is not clear. Many are attributed to David. Scholars tell us that a few may have been borrowed from the poems of neighboring peoples. But all 150 psalms were gathered together as the prayers of God's peculiar people. The longing they express for a relationship with God is never the prayer of a lone individual. Though deeply personal, psalms are never private. They are meant to be prayed in public for the sake of the whole people of God. The personal struggles they recount are burdens that God's people are always to bear together. And the delight they express is always to be the celebration of the assembly. The Psalter is a school not for individuals but for a people. To learn to pray the psalms is to become a member of God's holy people.

But we must always remember that our membership is a scandal. Indeed, the psalms themselves remind us that we are outsiders. They are poetry and, like any poetry, they must be read in the original language for their artistry to make sense. But these poems called psalms are all written in Hebrew. And who among us Gentiles really knows Hebrew? (I have studied Hebrew in the Gentile academies of America, but I would not dare say I know it. I could never write a poem or tell a joke in Hebrew.) Most of us who pray the psalms are dependent upon translations to have any sense of what is going on in them. Such dependence means that we are outsiders. The psalms are not only strange to us because they are the Word of God. They are doubly foreign because they are the prayers of a peculiar people called Israel.

So it is that we sometimes find ourselves genuinely unable to pray the Psalms as prayers of our own. We are embarrassed by their claims of innocence or appalled by their desire for vengeance. Though we read the Psalms morning and evening here at Rutba House, there are times when our community has to admit that *we* are not praying them. We cannot pray them because they are not our prayers. It is this realization that, Dietrich Bonhoeffer asserted, is our "first glimpse of the secret of the Psalter." In his book *Life Together*, a classic text on community, Bonhoeffer observed, "A psalm that we cannot utter as a prayer, that makes us falter and horrifies us, is a hint to us that here Someone else is praying, not we. . . .The *Man* Jesus Christ . . . is praying in the Psalter through the mouth of his Church. The Psalter is the prayer book of Jesus Christ in the truest sense of the word. He prayed the Psalter and now it has become his prayer for all time."[6]

So the problem of the psalms being both the Word of God and human words is solved christologically. The One who is both fully God and fully human prays the psalms for us, and we learn to pray them in him as living members of his body. It is only in Jesus, the son of a Jewish woman, that we can be counted with Israel, God's holy people. But, at the same time, it is only as Israel that we can claim to be a people with access to the inner life of God. In Jesus, by the power of the Spirit, we are caught up into God's life as a community. Where Father, Son, and Holy Spirit give themselves to one another in love, there our spirits join their never-ending dance. As with any dance, it is patient and persistent practice that makes us able to inhabit the mind of our Partner and follow his lead.

Patience and the Pursuit of God

Monastic wisdom teaches us that one of the most difficult things to overcome in the life of prayer is our disappointment with its banality. Thomas Merton, a Trappist monk who both popularized monasticism in America and befriended a circle of budding new monastics in the 60s, wrote in one of his journals: "all monasteries are more or less ordinary. The monastic life is by its very nature 'ordinary.'"[7] Merton's point was not to bemoan the banality of monastic life but rather to recognize it as a gift. It is precisely the ordinariness of the monastic life that makes true conversion possible. When a person is no longer distracted by the emotional illusions that passing trends and extraordinary events create, she has the opportunity to cultivate a life of the spirit. This opportunity is a gift. And it is a gift to be in a community where the life of the spirit is valued, and our individual desires are checked by people who know us well.

Recently, I was invited to apply for a job that I had not considered before. Though I didn't admit it to myself then, I think I was

[6] Bonhoeffer, *Life Together*, 45–46.

[7] Merton, *Sign of Jonas*, 20.

flattered by the invitation. The opportunity seemed exciting and out of the ordinary. I didn't say much about it to folks here in the community of Rutba House but agreed to meet with the person who had invited me to apply for the job. As I was washing dishes the morning of the meeting, a fellow community member asked me if I was coming to our scheduled vigil against the death penalty that day. "No," I said, "I have a meeting." I knew what was coming. "What kind of meeting?" That I didn't want to tell her should have told me something was wrong. When I did tell her about the job, she reminded me that I had said before, that I would never want a job like that. In short, she exposed my ego's desire for something extraordinary. This exposure wasn't any fun, but I believe it was a gift.

It is more than a coincidence, I think, that my desire to pursue something out of the ordinary conflicted with a vigil. Vigils are, after all, about watching and waiting for God to appear in the midst of the ordinary. Toward the end of Matthew's gospel, Jesus tells a parable about ten virgins. All ten of them were bridesmaids in a midnight wedding, waiting for the groom to arrive, so they could go to the wedding party. All ten had the desire to greet the groom and enjoy the party. All ten were virgins, pure and righteous. And all ten were human. When it got late, they all fell asleep.

Despite all that these ten virgins had in common, Jesus says that five of them were wise, and five were unwise, because when a shout woke them announcing the arrival of the bridegroom, only five still had enough oil in their lamps to keep the fire burning. "The foolish said to the wise, 'Give us some of your oil, for our lamps are going out.' But the wise replied, 'No! there will not be enough for you and for us; you had better go to the dealers and buy some for yourselves'" (Matt 25:8–9). This is not a problem of the haves and the have-nots. It is not as if there would have been enough oil to go around if everyone with oil had shared the portion given to her. No, if the wise virgins had shared their oil, everyone would have run out; which is to say, there would have been no wedding procession. So Jesus' parable of the ten virgins is a story about the way the Great Celebration of God's kingdom is dependent on something as ordinary as a few folks checking their oil.

But when we ask the question, who are the wise virgins? (*the question that a story like this compels us to ask*), our broken human condition is laid bare before us. We may, at times—after great sacrifices and years of constant devotion—be tempted to believe in our own purity. But in this story, all ten of the virgins were pure. Still, five did not have enough oil. Our purity does not make the kingdom party happen. We may then, in the face of our depravity, be tempted throw ourselves wholesale upon grace, confessing that we are "only human." But all ten virgins were human. They all fell asleep. Still, five of them were prepared for the late-night vigil. They had enough oil to keep their lamps burning until the bridegroom came.

The wisdom of salvation, it seems, rests on something as ordinary as having enough oil. If preparedness is as simple as that, though, why would anyone not be ready? Why do we burn our candles at both ends, chasing after extraordinary experiences—something more exciting than waiting on the Lord? Why do we use up all our oil trying to achieve the kingdom that is already among us, breaking forth in our midst? Why did I succumb to the temptation to chase after some better work than keeping vigil, something more extraordinary than waiting for the peace that I know in Christ to break through hardened hearts and to end the death penalty?

The trouble is that we are all unwise virgins. We are all unprepared to the extent that we do not believe our ordinary lives have been redeemed. We are not, for the most part, much impressed by incarnation. True, we celebrate Christmas each year and wonder at Immanuel, God with us. But we are ever prone to stress the extraordinary—the visitation of angels, the virgin birth, heralds from heaven, wise men from the East. All these astound us, and we long for an encore in our lives. But we move too fast to know our deepest longing—to know what poet-priest Dan Berrigan captures beautifully in his poem "Your Longing; Trivial Life Redeemed—'mysterium tremendum, Incarnation."

> Tremendum
> that God be
> ignorant from birth?
> And brawn of youth
> clumsy at start,
> bent thus and so
> to nicety

of joist and notch and beam?

Tremendum
        infused with trivial—
                a mewling infant
essays a first step, molds sounds
tantamount to words, grows confident.
An unsubmissive gaze at length
sizes the world,
finds to his eye, little at home
wanting, much alas abroad—
dire lack,
        illest luck. . . .[8]

That God in Jesus knows "dire lack, illest luck"—this is the tremendous mystery of the incarnation. Not so much that Jesus was born of a virgin, but that he was *born*, "a mewling infant." God makes himself ordinary like us. "In you and me / Himself discovers, in / mirrors of disbelief / and belief," Berrigan writes.[9] We are, all of us, unwise virgins. But because salvation is born as a baby who will grow up to give his body, broken for us, our trivial lives are redeemed. In Christ, the wisdom of God, we are made wise. Conversion is as ordinary and tremendous as incarnation: "Thus do great events and puny / mingle, make in total / mysterium tremendum, both."[10]

So the Apostle Paul prays at the beginning of his letter to the Ephesians that God would "give you a spirit of wisdom and revelation as you come to know him, so that, with the eyes of your heart enlightened, you may know the hope to which he has called you . . ." (Eph 1:17–18). Conversion of the spirit means patiently receiving Christ's wisdom—a wisdom that must be revealed—so that we learn to see with inner eyes the kingdom that we hope for. To be converted within is to have the eyes of our hearts enlightened such that we see a whole new world around us. But even as our minds are being transformed, we have to learn how to live with our bodies in the new

---

[8] Quotations from "Your Longing; Trivial Life Redeemed—'mysterium tremendum, Incarnation," are taken from correspondence with the author, September 9, 2005.

[9] Ibid.

[10] Ibid.

world we see. Conversion within is always simultaneously about conversion without. We turn to God to find a new way of life.

II. Catechesis and Conversion: What Turning Looks Like

To see how conformity to the mind of Christ within is tied to our outward way of life in community, it may be helpful to look closely at the prayer that Jesus taught his disciples to pray. It is the common prayer of every Christian community. After you've decided whether to say "debts" or "trespasses," you can recite it together with other believers in almost any congregation. The Lord's Prayer is a reminder that we Christians are a people who share in common, at the very least, a Father in heaven and a particular way of talking to God. The closer we look at this prayer, though, the more we see that being part of God's people looks like something. Faithfulness has a form (or forms), which can be seen because they are lived out by a community.

"Our Father, who art in heaven, hallowed be thy name," the prayer begins. Our first petition seems very "spiritual"—a request that God's name would be made holy. But to mention the holy name of God is to remember that this prayer grows out of the dusty soil of Mount Horeb, where Moses once saw a burning bush that was not consumed and heard a voice telling him to take off his shoes because he was standing on holy ground (Exod 3:5). On that soil Moses learned the holy name of God, YHWH—a name so holy that faithful Jews today do not speak it out loud. But Moses taught the Name to his people in Egypt, and he told Pharaoh that it was the Holy One who was going to lead his people out of Egypt into a Promised Land.

Back up on a desert mountain, Moses recognizes the voice of the Holy One when he hears it again, a second time. Only this time Moses has the people called Israel with him. The Holy One wants to give this people a law—to teach them how to live. But before YHWH can finish giving the law to Moses, the sounds of Israel worshiping other gods reach the mountaintop. YHWH, then, says to Moses, "I have seen this people, how stiff-necked they are. Now let me alone, so that my wrath may burn hot against them and I may consume them, and of you I will make a great nation" (Exod 32:9–10).

But Moses remembers that Israel bears the holy name of the Lord. And Moses remembers that he spoke that holy name to Pharaoh: "Why should the Egyptians say, 'It was with evil intent that he brought them out to kill them in the mountains, and to consume them from the face of the earth'?" (Exod 32:12). If Israel is destroyed, the Holy One's name will be mocked among the nations. The only way for the name of God to be made holy, then, is for God to make this people holy. So "the LORD changed his mind about the disaster that he planned to bring on his people" (Exod 32:14). On that day, the Holy One committed to make a people holy.

This is an important story for us to remember as we pray "hallowed be thy name. Thy kingdom come, thy will be done, on earth as it is in heaven." The holiness of God's name among the nations is inextricably tied to the existence of God's kingdom on earth among a people who are called by that name. This connection between God's holiness and God's reign in God's people is why the kingdom of God can be neither a solely spiritual reality within us nor an otherworldly hope for the future. The kingdom is a way of life that God has given to us now, "on earth as it is in heaven." Conversion is about learning to live in the new reality that Jesus's resurrection makes possible.

Kingdom Realism

When I took an introduction to philosophy class as an undergraduate, I learned the important modern distinction between realism and idealism. Idealism, the textbooks say, is about what can be imagined in theory. It is about the realm of ideas, far above the ground of the real world. Realism, on the other hand, is about what can be done in practice, here and now. While idealism may contribute to our reflections on what is possible in a given situation, realism dictates what responsible action looks like after all the possibilities have been considered. In short, realism always wins in the end.

Take war as an example. No one likes war. Ideally, we would always imagine alternative solutions to the problems between nations. In reality, however, wars must sometimes be fought. When all else fails (where "all else" means whatever alternatives the war-makers could imagine), war is the answer that realism offers. Indeed, realism says that it would be irresponsible not to fight a war if the threat against a people were greater than the anticipated harm of war.

According to the logic of realism vs. idealism, responsible people use lethal force to ensure justice when they can think of no other way to achieve peace.

In twentieth-century America, theologian and ethicist Reinhold Niebuhr popularized a position he called "Christian realism," essentially baptizing this modern logic of realism vs. idealism. Niebuhr argued that the Christian doctrine of original sin explained why ideal solutions are often simply unworkable in the real world. We cannot simply love everyone. To love our neighbor in a world broken by sin might mean killing the person who is trying to hurt our neighbor. Likewise, failure to kill the person if he could not be stopped otherwise would be a moral failure. Niebuhr was widely recognized in the mid-twentieth century as America's public theologian, and his way of thinking about Christian ethics became commonplace in U.S. churches. Even if you've never heard of Niebuhr, you've probably learned to think as he did.

Monasticism has always insisted that it is possible for real people to live the way that Jesus taught and practiced. Indeed, the wisdom of the monastic tradition teaches us a different logic than that which Niebuhr assumed in modern America. Instead of accepting the divide between realism and idealism, the monastic vision presents a conflict of realities that is taking place simultaneously on two planes, one spiritual and one material—in heaven and on earth. Just as we have seen that there is within each of us a conflict between our true self and our false self, so also we have to learn to see in the world around us a conflict between what Scripture calls "the kingdoms of this world" and "the kingdom of our God."

With the realists, Christian or otherwise, we acknowledge the deep brokenness of our world. Original sin does indeed mean that we have the potential for great evil, and history demonstrates our ability to realize that potential for evil. This reality does not change if we are nice or if we just love people or if we ignore it and pretend that it is not there. At the same time, however, we know that another reality is present in the world. It is not an ideal floating somewhere above the real world. God's kingdom exists alongside the broken kingdoms of this world.

In Matthew's Gospel Jesus tells the story of a farmer who sows wheat in his field. Sometime in the night an enemy comes behind him and sows weeds among the wheat (a story from the real world if ever there was one). The seeds grow into plants, and the field hands see what has happened. They report the weeds to the farmer and ask if they should tear out the weeds. But he says to them, "No; for in gathering the weeds you would uproot the wheat along with them. Let both of them grow together until the harvest; and at harvest time I will tell the reapers. Collect the weeds first and bind them in bundles to be burned, but gather the wheat into my barns" (Matt 13:29–30).

Jesus's parable teaches us the logic of competing realities. The weeds and the wheat grow up together in this world. Both are equally real. Both can be seen, touched, experienced. The weeds, however, are destined for destruction. Only the wheat will last. The reality we know as God's kingdom will last forever.

So in contrast to Niebuhr's "Christian realism," we have tried to develop an ethic of "Kingdom realism" at Rutba House. Our name comes from a town called Rutba in the western desert of Iraq. As members of a Christian Peacemaker Teams (CPT) delegation, my wife Leah and I went to Iraq at the beginning of Operation Iraqi Freedom in March 2003.When Saddam Hussein's government forced our delegation to leave, before the U.S. troops took Baghdad, we had to drive through the western desert while the area was being bombed by U.S. military planes. Just outside of Rutba, one of our cars hit a piece of shrapnel in the road and careered into a side ditch, seriously injuring two of our teammates. Our driver, however, did not immediately recognize that their car was no longer behind us. By the time we turned around to find them, our friends were gone. Their car had been left on its side in the ditch.

Shortly after the wreck, we later learned, a car of Iraqis had stopped by the roadside to help our bloody friends out of the ditch. They took them into their vehicle and carried them to Rutba. There a doctor told them, "Two days ago your country bombed our hospital, but we will take care of you because we take care of everyone. Muslim or Christian, Iraqi or American, we take care of everyone." He sowed up two of our friends' heads, saving their lives. By the time we caught up with them, they were resting in the beds of a makeshift clinic. I asked the doctor what we owed him for his services. "You do not owe me anything," he said. "Please just tell the world what has happened in Rutba."

As we told that story after returning to the United States, we realized that it was a modern-day Good Samaritan story. Just as the Samaritan, who was supposed to be the enemy of the Jews, had stopped by the roadside to help a battered Jewish man in Jesus's parable, so, too, had some Iraqis, who were supposed to be America's enemies, stopped by the roadside to save the lives of our American friends. It was not an ideal scenario imagined in some ivory tower. No, it had really happened to us in a place called Rutba.[11] The reality of God's kingdom had appeared in the midst of the broken reality of war-torn Iraq. By God's grace, we saw, it was possible to live the Kingdom's reality in this world. True, our story gave us only a glimpse—a single act by anonymous passersby and an Iraqi doctor who happened to speak perfect English. But we knew it was real. And if it was real, it could be lived out elsewhere at other times. We named our new monastic community Rutba House in hope that we could live out day to day the reality we had seen in Rutba. Kingdom realism meant believing that conversion could happen to us, right here in Walltown.

Joining a Tribe

What happened in Rutba was spectacular. It makes for a good story. But it's hard to know how that kind of radical hospitality translates into our everyday existence. We've had to ask the question, what made it possible for the folks in Rutba to be so compassionate toward us?

During World War II, the people of a small French town called Le Chambon-sur-Lignon provided sanctuary to Jews and other political refugees who fled from Nazi Germany. At least 2,500 people were saved by their hospitality. In his book *Lest Innocent Blood Be Shed*, Philip Hallie writes that when he went to Le Chambon to inquire about the sources of this incredible act of resistance, the people were universally convinced that they had done nothing extraordi-

[11] Wilson-Hartgrove, *To Baghdad and Beyond*.

nary. They could not have done otherwise, they insisted. It just made sense to take care of fellow human beings who were in need.[12]

For the people of Le Chambon, hospitality was a given. Somehow, it had become a way of life. Like the doctor in Rutba, they said, "We take care of everyone." They did not have to think about it. They did not have to rise above their normal practice at a crisis moment. Because hospitality was a given, they had only to be who they were. The very existence of a hospitable culture over and against Nazi Germany was itself a radical witness. What was crucial was the common culture of welcome that had been cultivated among the people.

John Alexander, who was for many years the pastor of the Church of the Sojourners community in San Francisco, once wrote an essay that he called the "Apache Document," proposing this scenario to his readers:

> Suppose a white person went to Arizona for a weekend and came back saying he'd become an Apache. He still talked the same, he still lived the same place, he still related to nature the same way, he still talked to everyone he saw, and he didn't spend much time with Apaches. The only change you could see was that he wore buckskin Sunday mornings and went around telling people he'd become an Apache.
>
> What would you think? I'd think it was odd. I'd suspect he hadn't joined the Apache tribe in any meaningful sense.[13]

Alexander's point, of course, was that we don't usually think about conversion as joining a tribe. Yes, we talk a good bit about conversion. And, yes, most Christians learn how to look like a Christian on Sunday mornings. But there is little evidence that most of American Christianity actually believes that the gospel offers us a new culture—a new ethnic identity in our sea of multiculturalism.

But if God really has made us part of a holy people, then we have been baptized into a new family whose way of living calls into question all the practices of our different cultures. This is not to say that black Christians have to become white or that Latinos need

---

[12] Hallie, "How Goodness Happened Here," 269–87.
[13] Alexander, "On Becoming an Apache."

to act black, but rather that black, white, and Latino must become Christian. First Christian, then white. First Christian, then black. First Christian, then Latino. For Christianity is a culture—a set of beliefs and stories and practices that shapes our vision of the world around us and the decisions we make about ways to act in the world. Christianity is not a culture wholly incompatible with black culture or with white American culture, with Hindu culture or with Arabic culture. But it is a culture that calls every human practice into question.

Take eating, for example. At Rutba House, we have people who come from a number of different cultures. It did not take us long to learn that we don't eat the same way. When Isaac from Southern California would make his tofu salad, Roy from Walltown would skip dinner. When Roy fried chicken, Isaac would eat it—and run to the bathroom afterwards. Finally, we decided that we needed to talk about our eating. Each person shared likes and dislikes, what each of us would eat and wouldn't eat. And then we sat there staring at each other. We were a mosaic of multiculturalism, but we couldn't figure out how to eat together.

Finally, someone suggested that we think about the Lord's Supper as a model for how Christians eat. This led to a Bible study in which we spent a couple of months talking and praying together about the way God's hospitality is made real around a dinner table, how care for creation is reflected in our food choices, how rich and poor are blessed together by a great feast where all are welcome, how we take care of each others' bodies by cooking nutritious meals.[14] We learned to see that there are ways to eat together as Christians that are more important than what any of us liked to cook or most enjoyed eating on our own. So some of us who used to be vegetarians now eat meat once or twice a week. And just the other day, I heard Roy say that he thought John's tortellini tasted better than fried chicken. (You may not realize what a conversion that is.) We haven't by any means figured out *the* Christian way to eat. But we have learned that our eating together is about serving Christ in one another. We've learned to ask how Christian eating is different from the eating we used to do.

[14] The workbook we used for our study was called "Just Eating?" I recommend it highly.

But culture is not just about eating. It really is about every part of our lives. We've had similar conversations about money, education, worship style, art, recreation, living spaces, family relations, work, dating, marriage, and sex. And maybe most importantly, we've talked about how to talk about these things like Christians.

Community decision-making is a practice for us. It is something we work on every week. After our check-in times, we have a community meeting each week. There we make decisions about our life together. Unlike a conventional church business meeting or PTA gathering, these community meetings are about things that most people think they can decide on their own (that is, until they fail miserably, at which point they usually consult a professional counselor). We talk about how we're going to spend our money, whom someone might want to date, whether to invite someone to live with us, or how to deal with a tension in a marriage. Everyone has a chance to address any agenda item. After everyone is heard, we work to find a decision that everyone can agree to support.

Majority rule is not good enough for our purposes. For most of us to force our will on a few would be a betrayal of the gospel in which the last are made first. But we cannot defer to the least common denominator either, deciding to do whatever no one objects to. All of us have submitted ourselves to the wisdom of the community. We have each asked the others to help us know the best thing to do. So no one has veto power. If everyone else tells me I should do something, my prior commitment to consensus means I need to choose to do it.

Now, this may seem like a lot of talk about how we talk about what we're going to do. I'll admit, we only decided to do it this way because someone we respected told us we should. But there was a point when I realized the wisdom of this process for myself. One day we had a fight in the community. I don't actually remember now what it was about, but I do recall people yelling in the living room and more than one person crying. It was bad. So we called an emergency community meeting. Everyone sat down in a circle, like we do every week. We went around the circle and listened to each person say what they thought had happened. Eventually, someone admitted they had been wrong and asked for forgiveness. We prayed together, and people embraced who, an hour before, had been yelling at one another.

When the meeting was over, I realized that real reconciliation had occurred in our living room. In another setting, someone might have called what we had just witnessed "nonviolent intervention." Had we invited in a professional mediator, it would have cost us hundreds of dollars to have such a helpful meeting. But as I reflected on the events of that evening, it occurred to me that we had been practicing for that meeting every Sunday evening. When our emotions were high, we didn't have to think about how to let everyone's voice be heard. We knew how to do it by habit. We knew because we had practiced community discernment and decision-making in our weekly meetings. The practice was second nature because consensus decision-making had become part of our common culture.

Culture cannot be learned in a weekend. That was the point John Alexander wanted to make with his Apache analogy. You can't become a Christian just by deciding you like the idea. It takes commitment to particular people in a particular place to learn a way of life. You have to stick around Christians for a while to even know what becoming a Christian would mean.

In the monastic tradition, that sticking around for a while is called a novitiate. Benedict knew that people could not just read his *Rule* and decide to follow it. They would have to practice living it with other people for a while before they could know what they were getting into. So he created a role called "novice" for people who wanted to learn the culture of the monastery.

> Let easy admission not be given to one who newly cometh to change his life; but, as the Apostle saith, "Try the spirits, whether they be of God" (1 Jn 4:1). If, therefore, the newcomer keepeth on knocking, and after four or five days it is seen that he patiently beareth the harsh treatment offered him and the difficulty of admission, and that he persevereth in his request, let admission be granted him, and let him live for a few days in the apartment of the guests.
>
> But afterward let him live in the apartment of novices, and there let him meditate, eat, and sleep. Let a senior also be appointed for him, who is qualified to win souls, who will observe him with great care and see whether he really seeketh

> God, whether he is eager for the Work of God, obedience
> and humiliations. Let him be shown all the hard and rugged
> things through which we pass on to God (RB 58:1–8).

Maybe four or five days of knocking seems a little harsh (and I'm
not sure what to do when you have an answering machine), but the
novitiate is a reminder that conversion is not as simple as saying you
want to become an Apache. It requires participation in a community.
Conversion does not happen to us on our own or all at once. It is
always about commitment to a community and its way of life.

All this tribal language will inevitably make some people ner-
vous. Sometimes people ask us, "If you say that someone has to commit to a community to learn how to be a Christian, aren't you saying
that you're the only Christians?" Not at all, we say. We are not the
only community of Christians. (And a community doesn't have to be
"neo-monastic" to be Christian.) But we do feel we've learned from
our experience that commitment to discerning how God is calling us
to live together has been essential to our conversion. No doubt other
communities have discerned much better than we have. But communities have to do it together. Conversion is the work of a tribe,
not of an individual.

Relocation and Renewal

If conversion requires a people, it also needs a place. This is why the
stability that Jon writes about in chapter four is so important. Our
life together in pursuit of God has to happen somewhere. "Location,
location, location," as they say in real estate. But the monastic wisdom about location seems to be the opposite of what a real estate
agent would tell you. Find a neighborhood where you can't convince
a realtor to show you anything, and you've probably found a place
where God is at work.

In Scripture, the wilderness is a wild and dangerous place. Jesus
is tempted by Satan there. Israel is doomed to wander there for forty
years because of its disobedience. But the wilderness also becomes
Israel's school. It is where God gives the law to his people. John the
Baptist goes to the wilderness to preach repentance and to announce
the arrival of God's kingdom in Jesus. The wilderness is not only an
abandoned space. It's also a place for renewal.

Monasticism has long recognized that relocation to abandoned places is an important part of conversion. The very first monks were called Desert Fathers and Mothers because they left the cities of the Roman Empire and went out into the Egyptian desert to wait on the Lord. There they found a renewed intimacy with God and, in the words of one historian, "the desert became a city."[15] In that formerly abandoned place, God's Spirit breathed on communities that offered their contemporaries a new way of life. The culture of that new community became a leaven for the church. It reminded the whole Christian community what they had been called to be in the world—a city set on a hill.

"Flee from the midst of Babylon," the prophet Jeremiah writes, "save your lives, each one of you! Do not perish because of her guilt, for this is the time of the Lord's vengeance; he is repaying her what is due" (Jer 51:6). In the book of Revelation, John returns to this biblical theme to stress the importance of relocation for our salvation (Rev 18:4). The trouble is not that God is absent from places of power and prestige, but rather that God is often judging people in those places for their injustice against the poor. When we flee to the abandoned places, we learn that God is there, with people we thought unimportant. But more, we learn who we are—a people dependent on God, in exile from our true home. We long to see God's holy city descend right here on earth as it is in heaven. Our longing is a reminder that Babylon, the earthly city, is not our home.

John Perkins, founder of the Christian Community Development Association (CCDA), has helped us understand the role relocation plays in conversion to God's beloved community. When people of privilege relocate to marginalized communities, Perkins says, we meet brothers and sisters in Christ who do not have access to the same resources we do. Compelled by God's desire for justice, those of us with access will redistribute resources, so that everyone has enough. If brothers and sisters who have suffered poverty are then willing to forgive those of us who had plenty, genuine reconciliation is possible. But these "three Rs" of community development—relocation, redistribution, and reconciliation—necessarily begin with relocation. It is the crucial first step. For us, it has made all the difference.

[15] Chitty, *Desert a City*.

When we first moved to Durham and sensed a call to the Walltown neighborhood, we couldn't find a house in Walltown large enough to host Rutba community. So we rented a place on the edge of Walltown in a much more upscale neighborhood. It was close enough that we walked to church in Walltown. I rode my bike through Walltown every day. But we never could convince anyone who lived in Walltown to come to our house for dinner. And when we had homeless guests from Walltown come to stay with us, they talked about how glad they were to have "made it out." We knew we had a problem when we realized that our hospitality had become a chance to get out of the hood and into the American dream.

So we started praying for a house in Walltown. But everything was still too small. Anything with more than three bedrooms had been turned into a duplex. We were praying for something that we knew didn't exist. Then one day, as Leah turned down a street she didn't usually drive on, she saw a "For Rent" sign in front of a house that sat off the road a bit, behind a tree. The sign said, "five bedrooms." When we called the owner, he told us he had just put the sign out that day. A month later, Rutba House moved into Walltown.

Two years after that move, I would say that it has contributed more to our community than any other single decision we've made. A commitment to this place has made conversion possible in ways we could not imagine just six blocks away. Making Walltown home has made this neighborhood's perspective, struggles, and joys our own. From here we have learned to see that this world is not our home. But we know that another world is possible, right here on earth. On good days, we see it—even around the dinner table.

Conclusion: Practicing Resurrection

Conversion is hard. On the inside, it means turning against your own will, learning to deny the false self and to find your true self in Christ. On the outside, it means turning away from the reality of this broken world, toward the reality of a kingdom that natural eyes often cannot see. Conversion means joining a contrast culture, going against the grain. This may sound radical and exciting to some, like indie music or WTO protests. What remains to be said, though, is that conversion means death. The way that Christ invites us to walk leads body and soul to a cross.

And death, however radical, is never fun. Dying is hard work. Especially in America. If there is any single myth that Christians must counter in American culture it is the optimistic tale of infinite progress beyond death. "Americans like to appear as if they give death hardly any thought at all," wrote theologian Arthur McGill. "Of course, death will happen to all of us someday, but until then, it is not something to think about or grapple with. Until then our preoccupation should be with life and with all of its challenges and adventures. Let the dying deal with death. Our calling is to enjoy life."[16] Conversion in this culture is about learning to see, as Thomas Merton said, that "we are involved in a struggle between love and death, and this struggle takes place within each of us."[17] Turning to the God who is our life, we learn to see death as a daily reality rooted deep in our souls and daily practices. But it is a reality we no longer have to avoid. In Christ, death has been defeated.

One of the "instruments of good works" for St. Benedict is "to keep death before one's eyes daily" (RB 4:47). Conversion is facing death head on. "Community life is like martyrdom by fire," wrote Eberhard Arnold, founder of the Bruderhof communities. "It means the daily sacrifice of all our strength and all our rights, all the claims we commonly make on life and assume to be justified. In the symbol of fire the individual logs burn away so that, united, its glowing flames send out warmth and light again and again into the land."[18] In the end, conversion is about being consumed by the fire of God's love so that the whole world might know his glory. By fire we are transformed, joined to one another and to God at the same time. "It is an exceedingly dangerous way," Arnold warns. Conversion is not easy. "And yet, just this is our deepest joy: to see clearly the eternal struggle—the indescribably tension between life and death, . . . [humanity's] position between heaven and hell—and still to believe in the overwhelming power of life, the power of love to overcome, and the triumph of truth, because we believe in God."[19]

Thus dying, we see. Seeing, we believe. Believing, we turn. And turning, we live even though we die. "For I am crucified with Christ,

[16] McGill, *Death and Life*, 13.
[17] Merton, "Building Community on God's Love," 34.
[18] Arnold, "Why We Live in Community," 14.
[19] Ibid., 2.

and it is no longer I who live, but Christ lives within me. And the life I now live in the flesh I live by faith in the Son of God, who loved me and gave himself for me" (Gal 2:20). To be converted is to practice resurrection, inside and out.

3

Obedience

Tim Otto

ONE OF THE STORIES that gets told in my family is of my uncle, who at age eighteen had his third vehicle accident. In spite of many warnings by his devout Baptist parents, he drank a lot and drove his car fast. His third accident took place when he and a drunken friend drove off the road in his '54 Chevy and hit a tree. My uncle broke both his legs, his left arm, his collarbone, and put his head through the windshield. He found himself lying in a hospital bed with two leg casts, an arm cast, and a bandaged skull. His mother, usually one of the gentlest and most compassionate people to walk the earth, visited him in the hospital. She walked into the room, and surveying the state of her son, she said to him a succinct version of Psalm 107: "Son, the way of a transgressor is rough!" And then she walked out.

In spite of my grandmother's well-chosen words at the right moment, my uncle did not immediately become an obedient son. For some time, he continued on the "rough" way. Obedience has been hard in every age, and the simple wisdom of obedience is perhaps especially hard for modern people. Poet Percy Bysshe Shelley had this to say about obedience:

> Bane of all genius, virtue, freedom, truth,
> Makes slaves of men, and of the human frame
> A mechanized automaton.[1]

In our guts, we modern folk might find ourselves agreeing with his sentiments: obedience turns us back into ignorant children.

St. Benedict had a very different view of obedience. Following the writers of the wisdom literature in the Bible, Benedict saw obedience as the way to God. Like Augustine before him, St. Benedict didn't write a helpful handbook for happiness but rather a rule. It begins this way:

[1] "Queen Mab," III.178–80 in Shelly, *Complete Poetry*, 187.

> Listen, O my son, to the teachings of your *master*, and turn
> to them with the ear of your heart. Willingly accept the
> advice of a *devoted father* and put it into action. Thus you
> will return by the labor of obedience to the one from whom
> you drifted through the inertia of disobedience. Now then
> I address my words to you: whoever is willing to renounce
> self-will and take up the powerful and shining weapons of
> obedience to fight for the Lord Christ, the true King. (italics
> added)[2]

How many people would Benedict be addressing today? St. Benedict's opening paragraph is a tough hurdle for most modern readers, especially if we realize that with the words "master" and "devoted father" Benedict was not asking his readers to be directly obedient to God but to the abbot of each monastery.[3] Benedict thought that obedience to other human beings is crucial for spiritual health. If we are to learn from St. Benedict, who made obedience part of the threefold promise of monks, we've got to grapple with obedience. Why do we find it so hard? Why does Benedict see it as so essential?

These may be important questions at the right moment because many of us find ourselves in a kind of spiritual hospital bed. These might be worthwhile questions for many of us since, like my uncle, we often find ourselves off the narrow road, crashing our lives into trees of materialism, apathy, nationalism, or lust, and a host of other hazards. I suspect that if St. Benedict were to survey our lives, he might be tempted to say some version of "Sons and daughters, the ways of transgressors are rough."

Would he be right? And if so, what might obedience look like for us? And, again, if obedience promises us any kind of cure, why is it so hard to swallow?

An Incontinent Augustine

In order to understand Benedict's enthusiasm for obedience, it is important to understand Augustine, from whom Benedict inherited the idea of a rule. Augustine, after a decades-long argument with his mother, Monica, eventually concluded that his mother was right and

---

[2] Kardong, *Benedict's Rule*, 3.

[3] Ibid., 6.

wrote a thirteen-chapter book called *The Confessions*. In it, Augustine laid out the background for why he came to see obedience as so important. Augustine told of being caught between the goods and goals of his culture (advocated by his father), such as status, money, and pleasure, and the goal that his mother urged him toward: the love of God.

Augustine diagnosed himself with the disease of dispersion. It was not that he had no interest in God; he did. But Augustine also wanted status, money, and sex. Augustine would have argued that, at least in part, we find obedience so hard because we want so many things at once. My uncle, for instance, may have wanted to please his wise and loving mother, but he also wanted to fit in with other guys his age, to feel the high of intoxication, and to drive his Chevy fast.

Because we all have multiple loves and desires, Augustine thought that we all end up feeling scattered, fragmented, disjointed, ill at ease, and restless. For this reason, a key concept for Augustine was continence (meaning "the ability to release a bodily discharge voluntarily") not from the bladder, but from the will.[4] He thought of the will as leaking an "oozy discharge" as it pursues dozens of good and bad things all at the same time (*Conf.* 8.7.18). Augustine explained that, "By continence the scattered elements of the self are collected and brought back into the unity from which we have slid away into dispersion . . ." (*Conf.* 10.29.40). Continence enables the will to be directed toward a single goal. The title of a much later book from Søren Kierkegaard approaches the definition of continence: "Purity of heart is to will one thing."[5]

And what is the one thing? In Augustine's famous words at the very beginning of *The Confessions,* "You arouse us so that praising you may bring us joy, because you have made us and drawn us to yourself, and our heart is unquiet until it rests in you" (*Conf.* 1.1.1). We may long for dozens of things. In the song "Lord of the Starfields," contemporary songwriter Bruce Cockburn rephrases Augustine's famous words, noting that all our longings find their goal in God. Human beings have a goal, an end, a *telos.* We are made to praise and rest in God. For Augustine, holiness meant wholeness. As we are "set apart"

---

[4] "Continence," Merriam-Webster Online. http://m-w.com/dictionary/continence
[5] Kierkegaard. *Purity of Heart.*

(holy) for and to God, our scattered selves are gathered up and we become whole. This is what health looks like for all us humans who suffer the disease of dispersion.

It is important to notice how this conception of holiness differs from the popular understanding of holiness as "being good." Holiness is not moral perfection; holiness is resting in God. Holiness has less to do with being righteous than with trusting God. Holiness is less an abstract moral quality than it is a description of a relationship. Holiness means giving oneself wholly to God.

Although few of us wake up in the morning thinking, "I sure would like to be holy today," Augustine would have argued that holiness is actually our deepest desire. It is when we are holy that we are most content and happy. If we would be holy, we would no longer be pulled apart by our many loves and desires. It would be like a lover caught up in one great love, our entire being radiating a passionate joy in pursuing and serving the beloved. In Augustine's well-known prayer that begins, "Late have I loved you . . ." (*Conf.* 10.27.38), he writes that God attracted him like a lover. Speaking to God as if to a lover, Augustine says, [You] "shouted . . . flared, blazed, . . . and lavished your fragrance." In response, Augustine "gasped, [and now] I pant . . . I tasted you." In response to God's touch, Augustine "burn[s]." Immediately following this prayer, Augustine imagines that he will be completely alive and happy when he is completely filled with God (*Conf.* 10.28.39).

It may seem strange to modern people that Augustine suggests we enter into this great love through obedience. But for Augustine, the logic seemed straightforward. If our problem is that we are scattered, obedience has the possibility of unifying us in two ways. First, by our joining a community of those who have given up worldly things, our wills turn away from those things that distract us from God. Second, by communal disciplines such as fasting, prayer, and meditation, our wills are actively turned towards God. Notice again that the object here is not so much moral perfection as it is God. Augustine believed that through obedience, in the context of community, holiness—being completely given over to God—is possible.

The question arises for some of us, though, is what Augustine suggested scriptural? Was Augustine thinking biblically when he suggested that our end is holiness, and that we get there through a communal obedience?

Our End and How We Get
There according to Scripture

"What is the purpose of the Torah—the books of the law—Genesis through Deuteronomy?" One of the best answers might be, "they are meant to create a holy people."[6] God did not bring the people of Israel out of Egypt simply to be free. After liberating the people, God brought them to Mount Sinai and gave them the law, announcing, "Now therefore, if you obey my voice and keep my covenant, you shall be my treasured possession out of all the peoples. Indeed, the whole earth is mine, but you shall be for me a priestly kingdom and a holy nation" (Exod 19:5–6). The emphasis here is not so much on obedience making Israel good as it is on obedience making Israel God's.

The law, given at Sinai, included everything from the proper handling of cooking pots, to right relations with one's neighbor, to mandating frequent parties. The law was not meant to be a vast cobweb of "do-nots" to entangle or to trip up people but rather a way of "setting apart" humans for their true purpose: fellowship with God and participation in God's purposes. The law was almost always concerned with right relationship to God, others, oneself, and the land. In the Ten Commandments, the first four commandments have to do with right relationship to God, while the last six are directed toward right relationship with one's neighbor.

This emphasis on relationship ought not to be surprising for Christians. One of the hardest struggles for the church has been how to think about a God who is three persons yet perfectly one. God lives in perfect community. Given that, it makes sense that God would wish us to live in unity as well, both with one another and with God. To live well with one another and God does involve being good. But "being good" is a means to the end rather than the end itself. For instance, we are told not to steal. This commandment against stealing did not arise because God created an arbitrary moral category called "stealing" and then prohibited us from doing it. Rather, the

---

[6] Lohfink, "Torah as Social Project," 74.

commandment arose because stealing disrupts community. Stealing usually means thinking that something other than God is going to make one content.[7] So we are commanded not to do it.

In the context of the law being given, one of the exhortations to holiness is found in Deuteronomy 18:13, which says, "You must be blameless before the LORD your God." The Hebrew word for "blameless" in that verse also has the connotation of being "complete." It is probably this verse that Jesus picked up on in Matthew 5:48 when he said, "Be perfect, therefore, as your heavenly Father is perfect." The Greek word *teleios*, in addition to the meaning "perfect" or "blameless" also carries the connotations of "complete," "whole," and "end." Augustine's notion that our end is to become whole by being holy is consistent with the biblical witness. Was Augustine right, however, that the goal of holiness is achieved through obedience to rules?

Jesus said the words "be perfect" in the context of the Sermon on the Mount. Matthew seems to be intentionally presenting Jesus as the new Moses interpreting the law given on Mount Sinai. Jesus said something that may sound strange, at least to Protestant ears:

> For truly I tell you, until heaven and earth pass away, not one letter, not one stroke of a letter, will pass from the law until all is accomplished. Therefore, whoever breaks one of the least of these commandments, and teaches others to do the same, will be called least in the kingdom of heaven; but whoever does them and teaches them will be called great in the kingdom of heaven. (Matt 5:18–19)

Jesus went on to give very concrete commandments and rules: not only do not murder, but also do not insult a brother or sister; not only do not commit adultery, but also do not lust; not only love your neighbor, but also love your enemy as well. Imagine the extraordinary community-building power of these rules if they were followed!

Those are hard rules, and throughout the ages the church has found ways to explain them away. But we ought to be wary of such attempts. Jesus ended the Sermon on the Mount with a parable of wise and foolish builders. The wise man hears Jesus's words and puts

---

[7] Another impulse may underlie stealing in cases of real need. But in that case, stealing usually points to issues of justice in the community, issues that other laws address.

them into practice. The foolish man does not, and "great was the fall of his house" (Matt 8:27). Jesus told us to be holy—"perfect," even—and then gave us rules to help us achieve that. In Matthew's Gospel, Jesus's parting words to his disciples tell them to make disciples of all nations, "teaching them to obey everything that I have commanded you" (Matt 28:20).[8]

From start to finish the New Testament is filled with instructions, directions, teachings, and even commands to help us toward our end of holiness. Obedience is part of what the New Testament writers intend. Augustine's emphasis on obedience as the way to holiness is well attested by Scripture.

I certainly don't mean to put anyone in the torturous position that Martin Luther found himself in, thinking that he had to keep a list of rules to merit God's grace. Obeying the rules of the Bible is not a way of meriting God's love or grace. Rather, obedience is a way to move toward our created purpose. The rules are signposts and way-markers pointing to how to live in union with God and one another.

Anyone who has made a serious attempt at "being good" can probably relate to Luther's experience. If we are honest, we will eventually admit that becoming "holy" in the sense of "morally perfect" is impossible. If we think that moral perfection is what God demands, then we are setting ourselves up for discouragement and failure. So it is helpful to understand holiness primarily in terms of being given over to God rather than in terms of moral perfection.

Another way into this matter of holiness is to consider the frequent Old Testament admonition to be holy as God is holy (Lev 11:44–45; 19:2; 20:26; 21:8). On hearing this admonition to holiness, many of us, I suspect, think of holiness in terms of absolute goodness and purity. Enlightenment philosopher Immanuel Kant defined holiness as "the absolute or unlimited moral perfection of

---

[8] For those of us who have been raised on Luther's "justification by faith alone," this may seem a terrible misunderstanding of the New Testament. We've been taught to label such teaching as "works righteousness." A full discussion of "works righteousness" is well beyond what I'm able to do here. One simple comment is that even if Luther was completely right about justification, justification is not the ultimate purpose of humans. Even if faith is all we need to be justified, God doesn't want us just to "make it into heaven." God wants us to be complete, whole, healthy, entire, and, well, holy.

the will."[9] Such language, however, is mostly foreign to the Bible. As theologian John Webster points out, in the biblical witness,

> [t]he holiness of God is not to be identified simply as that which distances God from us; rather, God is holy precisely as the One who in majesty and freedom and sovereign power bends down to us in mercy. God is the Holy One. But he is the Holy One 'in your midst', as Hosea puts it (Hos. 11:9); or as Isaiah puts it: 'great in your midst is the Holy One of Israel' (Isa. 12:6).[10]

Webster makes the case that God's holiness is depicted not so much as a quality of God as an action of God toward the good of people. God's holiness has to do with God's desire to live with us. In the Bible, God's holiness often refers to God's actions to help the living-together happen.

The Context of Community

Augustine argues that our true home is holiness and that obedience is the road we walk to get there. Augustine established a monastery in Thagaste, North Africa, for himself and his friends, believing that the road of obedience is best walked with others. If obedience to rules helps create community with God and with one another, then perhaps Augustine's third claim—that obedience must take place in community—makes more sense. Augustine's logic finds good biblical support. Toward the beginning of the Sermon on the Mount (right after the Beatitudes), Jesus says, "You are the light of the world" (Matt 5:14). In Sunday school, I grew up singing, "This little light of *mine*, *I'm* going to let it shine." While this song is a lot of fun, it is theologically dangerous. The "you" in Jesus's sentence is a plural *you*, as in *y'all*. As if Jesus knew that we moderns wouldn't understand that he was referring to the community of disciples, his next line is, "A city on a hill cannot be hid." It is together—like those who live in a city—that we are to be a light to the world. Jesus was reminding Israel of its call: to be a light to the nations by being a holy, gathered people.

---

[9] Kant, "Lectures," 409.

[10] Webster, *Holiness*, 45.

Much of the rest of the New Testament is devoted to forming communities of obedience called churches. Many of the letters to churches start out with a greeting to the "saints," which is another way of saying "holy ones." In the opening greeting to the churches in Rome and Corinth, Paul writes to those "called to be saints/holy ones." Paul then goes on to give concrete teachings on ways people of those churches might live into their calling. Throughout the New Testament, the usual place for obedience to be worked out is in the context of a community called *church*. Augustine was right that obedience is not an individual project.

In spite of good biblical evidence for the truth of Augustine's belief that our *telos* (goal or end) is holiness and that we reach our *telos* through obedience in the context of a community, I suspect that many of us still have a good deal of apprehension and suspicion about the project of obedience. Augustine would have said that we struggle with obedience because we are unwilling to give up all desires other than our desire for God. Augustine had delayed converting to Christianity for many years because he didn't want to give up concupiscence, that is, all that delighted his senses—especially sexual love. Perhaps most of us have our own version of "concupiscence" that we are hanging on to.

Suspicions about Obedience

There are, however, historical reasons for moderns being more suspicious of obedience than were the ancients. We cannot ignore the long record of the ways authority has been abused and obedience coerced. From the Crusades, to the Inquisition, to the religious wars in Europe, even to the more contemporary figures of Jim Jones and David Koresh, we have too many appalling examples of the ways religious authority can be used to debase, demean, and destroy human beings.

Partly in response to that history, thinkers during the time of the Enlightenment began to question the assumptions of the "Christian culture."[11] As Alasdair MacIntyre narrates in his book *After Virtue*,

[11] The degree to which the Enlightenment was a response to that history is debatable. To at least some extent, Enlightenment propaganda itself suggests that the Enlightenment was born out of a response to abuses of religious authority. For instance, historian William Cavanaugh has argued that the "religious wars" of

faith in any kind of *telos* for human beings was shaken during the Enlightenment. After having celebrated reason's ability to criticize traditionalism, people realized that reason alone could not provide any ultimately convincing account of our purpose as humans. Many attempts were made to find such an account, and one such attempt resulted in the theory of utilitarianism. Humans were said to be those beings whose purpose was to "maximize the good and minimize harm." Such theories claimed to be rational and objective, but it quickly turned out that words such as *good* and *harm* only seemed rational and objective as long as the person advocating utilitarianism could define them. For instance, even if I were to define my good as being perpetually high on crack cocaine, my housemates might have another opinion of what my good should be. In the end, theories such as utilitarianism turned out to be as subjective as the religious traditions that they claimed to better.

Since western thinkers could no longer agree on where we were going, it became odd to take directions from others as to how to get there. Without any agreed on destination for humans, a theory called emotivism explains why human continue to busily give each other directions. Emotivism holds that "all evaluative judgments and more specifically all moral judgments are *nothing but* expressions of preference, expressions of attitude or feeling, insofar as they are moral or evaluative in character."[12] This served to focus attention on the motivations and interests of the one making judgments and issuing commands. As John R. Snyder explains the perspective of European nihilism, "All thought that pretends to discern truth is but an expression of the will-to-power—even to domination—of those making the truth claims over those who are being addressed by them."[13]

Since edicts, commands, directives, and instructions by kings, priests, and lords were no longer seen as necessarily sponsored by God, it became easier to see the self-interest and will to power that often motivated calls to obedience. Eventually, colonialism was called into question, as was slavery and the lack of equal rights for women.

Europe were, in fact, the birth pangs of nation-states and were billed as religious wars to justify the emerging power of the nation-state. See Cavanaugh, "Killing for the Telephone Company," 243–74.

[12] MacIntyre, *After Virtue*, 12.

[13] Snyder, "Translator's Introduction," xxi.

Liberation movements of all kinds flourished. It became possible to see the ways that misused authority had mangled and degraded many millions of lives.

The social sciences made more visible psychological, social, and political factors motivating calls to obedience. So today, churchgoers might wonder, "Is my pastor's call for faithful church attendance really for my good, or is it mostly to bolster the pastor's self-esteem by having full worship services?" Or, we might ask, "Was Augustine's attitude toward sex a true consequence of his desire for holiness in himself and others, or was his attitude toward sex a result of guilt inflicted on him by his mother?" We are now acutely aware of the potential for those who call for obedience to act in their own interest and out of their capacity to oppress others. Because we are suspicious of the motivations of those who call for obedience, we moderns have developed a kind of allergic reaction to the very idea of obedience.

Ancient Safeguards

It is important to note, however, that the ancients were not oblivious to the possible dangers of obedience. The church had at least two important safeguards for those entering communities of obedience. First, the church asked people to be obedient to those who were clear about the *telos* of humans. In ancient times, unlike in our own day, a supermodel could not just write a book, claiming to be "life coach and spiritual advisor." It is no accident that both Augustine and Benedict were eventually recognized as saints. Abbots and abbesses were chosen because they were widely recognized as having made progress toward a truly holy life. They would not be false guides leading people toward good looks, status, power, or money. These people were clear that the goal of life is God. Because of their real holiness, and the accompanying diminishment of their impure motives, abbots and abbesses could be trusted.

Second, abbots and abbesses were to have a kind of parental concern for those in their care. The first sentence of St. Benedict's section on "the qualities of the abbot" reads, "To be qualified to govern a monastery an abbot should always remember what he is called (*Abba* = Father) and carry out his high calling in everyday life." Benedict goes on to discuss the fatherly qualities that an abbot should possess. The abbot should demonstrate with "deeds, more than by words, what is good and holy." The abbot should show no partiality, and while exercising good discipline, the abbot should show the "love and affection of a father" (RB 2).[14] Also, like any good father, the abbot must take into account the different temperaments of the monks and treat them accordingly.

The church was seen to be so important that certain members did not marry in order to give themselves entirely to the church family. It was understood that whereas most people might pour their love into their biological children, those who dedicated themselves to the church would pour their love into spiritual children instead. Those entering monasteries and convents did so knowing that they were putting themselves in the position of being loved by holy people.

A Modern Obedience

In my own life, I have had an experience I imagine bears some relation to the experience of those who entered monasteries and convents in Benedict's day. I am the son of missionaries, and I attended a Christian college. Growing up in a Christian family, I saw the good of what obedience to loving parents might accomplish. In the church and in my Christian college, however, I went through various discipleship classes and programs. Each offered information that I was supposed to learn and practices that were supposed to improve my spiritual life. Perhaps I was just a poor student, but I rarely felt that I was experiencing the kind of transformative discipleship described in the New Testament directly as a result of the classes and programs I was attending.

A couple years after graduating from college, I moved into a Christian community called the Church of the Sojourners, a group that included children and older adults. I especially appreciated three of the older men in the community. They had structured their lives so that they had time to teach me, talk with me, and argue with me. I knew that they cared about me, and for the first time I felt that I was being "discipled" in the New Testament sense of the word. During my college experience, I had been in a generational ghetto of my peers, with the Church of the Sojourners I found that my elders, who had pursued holiness, had goods to share. In retrospect I sup-

[14] Meisel and del Maestro, *Benedict's Rule*, 48–50.

pose I became "obedient" to them. I made a promise to stick around and make the major decisions of my life with them and with others. I prayed with them; I sought out their wisdom; I tried to follow their instructions. And ultimately, this process was wonderful. It seemed to me that I was living the discipleship described by Jesus.

It wasn't that the process was always pleasant, or that my advisors made no mistakes along the way. In the end, though, this discipleship was a participation in a lineage of love. The Enlightenment has taught us to call such love a dangerous "paternalism." The Enlightenment would have us believe that being free individuals is in some sense our *telos*. Because of that Enlightenment influence, we've come to see the love of others as an emotion that we are to enjoy but that also ought to make us completely free to do whatever our hearts lead us to do. Augustine might have argued that such a love is its own kind of authoritarian socialization that makes us into slaves of our incontinent and tyrannical wills.

The assumption of the Enlightenment tradition that we can love children, or anyone else, toward an "objective" or "neutral" space, is mistaken. To form our children, or anyone else, into such a "neutral" space, would simply mean that we had formed them in the Enlightenment tradition. The Enlightenment tradition, like the Christian tradition, is accepted by faith, after all. But following Jesus's instruction to know teachers by their fruits, we can evaluate teachers, and perhaps even a tradition, by the fruit that it produces in people's lives (Matt 7:15–17). Believing that our Christian tradition has produced good fruit like that mentioned in Galatians 5:22–23 ("love, joy, peace, patience, kindness, generosity, faithfulness, gentleness, and self-control"), we can seek to love in a way that is more than a passing on of warm emotions. With our love, we can strive to participate in and even to contribute to a tradition with its own politics, social structure, art, and language, thereby creating a tradition designed to bless those who embrace it. For Christians, that tradition is called the church. Believing our tradition to be a source of truth and blessing, we want to be "obedient to" (meaning something akin to "loved by") its best practitioners. This desire to be "obedient to" and "loved by" the church is what I take to be the impetus behind "the new monasticism." It is the desire to be loved by the best lovers.

It is the desire to reach our true end. And it is the desire to contribute to a tradition that loves others yet to come.

St. Benedict's rule, following the insights of Augustine, serves as a good foundation for this project of the new monasticism. As Michael Cartwright has warned, we moderns might be tempted to "shop" the rule, meaning that we might adopt those aspects of it that we find attractive but leave the rest. If we are truly to apprentice ourselves to what St. Benedict had to offer, we must find a way of incorporating obedience into our lives. I've tried to show that obedience is an essential and deeply biblical component of discipleship. Augustine and Benedict highlighted something of great importance from Scripture, and yet we cannot ignore the insight of the Enlightenment: authority can be used to oppress and diminish others.

As modern Christians who seek to live faithfully yet who carry the cautions of the Enlightenment embedded in our hearts and souls, how can we live obediently? One story that has helped me think about living obediently in the present day is Chaim Potok's novel, *My Name is Asher Lev.*

The Struggle of Asher Lev

My Name is Asher Lev is the story of someone who loves his tradition and his people, someone who struggles hard to live within his tradition, and yet someone who ultimately is alienated from it. As a friend once said, "I know so many Asher Levs." For some of us, Asher Lev may represent ourselves—a person who has struggled to be obedient to a faith tradition and yet wonders if the tradition is stifling the very person that God made us to be.

Potok's novel tells the story of Asher Lev, a boy who grows up within a very tight-knit Jewish community in Brooklyn. He loves drawing, but at age six he grows frustrated while trying to draw his mother. He notices that the pencil he is using cannot capture all the shades of shadow on his mother's face. He finds that by using the ash from his mother's ashtray, he can create a closer likeness to his mother. Watching Asher do this, his father seems "awed and angry and confused and dejected, all at the same time."[15] Asher's father does not understand or appreciate Asher's gift.

---

[15] Potok, *My Name is Asher Lev*, 34.

As Asher grows, his early promise comes to fruition, and he becomes famous as an artist. But his community feels disgraced by him. As Asher laments on the first page of the novel, people are saying that he is a "traitor, an apostate, a self-hater, an inflictor of shame upon my family, my friends, and my people."[16] Asher's artistic path has led him to use nudes and crucifixes in his art, and his community cannot comprehend these choices. So although Asher loves his community, in the end he leaves his family, his friends, and his people.

My Name is Asher Lev is a retelling of the Enlightenment story. The Enlightenment story asserts that traditions such as Judaism or Christianity are finally unable to receive the unique gifts that each of us are, and in the end, the traditions are oppressive. Chaim Potok does, however, offer us an important help. He makes clear that Asher is not choosing between Judaism and being true to himself. Asher is choosing between traditions. As Jacob Kahn, Asher's art mentor, warns him, art "is a tradition; it is a religion . . . its values are goyisch and pagan."[17] Asher doesn't start painting nudes and crucifixes because they spontaneously combust within him and flow out of his heart and move through his fingers and brush onto canvas. Asher paints them because he has chosen to apprentice himself to a long line of artists who use those forms. Asher learns from his mentor and others that his deepest duty to express the "scream" that is in him with whatever forms best express that. In explaining art to his father, Asher says, "It's a person's private vision expressed in aesthetic forms."[18]

Asher's account of art differs from how many throughout history have understood art, except after the Enlightenment. For most of human history, artists have been seen as servants of the public rather than the personal—usually through creating art for communal events and ceremonies. As Bruce Benson points out, Mozart ate with the Archbishop of Salzburg's valets and cooks.[19] It was only after Enlightenment philosopher Kant that art was seen as having a purpose other than serving the community. Kant argued that art is to "have no purpose, except that of exciting the imagination in

---

[16] Ibid., 3.

[17] Ibid., 213.

[18] Ibid., 303.

[19] Benson, "Tearing Down the Wall," 45.

contemplating an artistic object."[20] Kant helped father an artistic tradition in which art is done "for art's sake," and its relevance to the community's goals are mostly seen as unimportant.

Another possibility does exist for Asher Lev. He could choose to be an artist who accepts the goals of his Jewish community rather than the goals of the post-Kantian artistic community. As Asher's father often reminds him, the goal of Asher's Jewish community is to make the world holy. That is not a bad goal. Maybe it is a better one than expressing one's own personal scream. For Asher to work as an artist within the worldview of his community would be difficult but not impossible. He probably would not gain much fame in New York art galleries. But if he succeeded . . . well, he might just help make the world more holy.

Realizing that Asher is choosing between traditions is important because Asher's choice illustrates that the choice we all have is not really a choice between a tradition and being true to oneself. We have no formed, autonomous self to be true to. There is only a choice between traditions. Bob Dylan's line, "ya gotta serve somebody" is profoundly true. The "choice" to be obedient or not is no choice at all. The only choice is to whom we are going to be obedient. This is one of the most crucial realizations concerning obedience. We will be, and already are, obedient. The question is only, to what tradition will we be obedient? Knowing this, it becomes possible to think about goals of the traditions that vie for our obedience.

Expressive Individualism

I suspect that *My Name is Asher Lev* resonates with so many people because it presents the alternative tradition that lives within most of us Westerners. Expressive individualism is not just for artists anymore. As Robert Bellah and his collaborators show in the book *Habits of the Heart,* a commitment to expressing ourselves is one of the most ingrained values of Westerners. Because of a history which includes the Enlightenment, the romantic thinkers, Freud, the human potential movement, the forces of a market economy, and a host of other factors, the ultimate use of our Western freedoms is, in

[20] Ibid., 49.

Bellah's words, "to cultivate and express the self and explore its vast social and cosmic identities."[21]

That may sound like a very grand and creative project. Perhaps it can be. For the artists who do it creatively or beautifully or provocatively, we've created sacred spaces called art museums where we venerate their work. For other types of artists, we've created performance art spaces, record labels, and movie studios. For the very best expressers of self, we've commoditized their expressions, and we can buy them at market prices to outfit our own expression of self.

Most of us however, are not producing for the local museum of modern art. For most of us, just as Asher's tradition offered him the forms of nudes and crucifixes with which to express himself, our market economy offers us the form of consumption as a way of expressing ourselves. I can buy shoes with swooshes on them to let myself and others know that I'm the kind of person who "just does it." Shopping for a vehicle, I can select the perfect combination of performance, style, and comfort to reflect my individuality. I can buy ringtones for my cell phone that scream "me!" and cell phone faceplates that mirror my self-image. Even such virtual entities as web logs and Internet profiles, which would seem to be pure expressions of the self, are often catalogs of what we consume. In an article titled "Me Media, one student agonizes over his music preferences on the website *Facebook*: "'I never used to update [my musical preference list], thinking it was just too fraught a category . . . I'm a musician: what I play and listen to has always been an important part of my identity, and it's only fairly recently that I've developed the confidence to say, you know, I like this, and I don't really care if you don't. So what's there now? Albums by Babyshambles, Lady Sovereign, Marxy, and My Bloody Valentine . . .'"[22]

I find that many of my conversations with friends have to do with what we've consumed lately—what books we've read, what movies we've seen, and what songs we've been listening to. Interestingly, many of those books, movies, and songs, tell us the story of how we need to be listening to our hearts and expressing our individuality. And the way our culture teaches us to do this is through buying more books, movies, and songs. As individuals, we become remarkably

---

[21] Bellah, et al, *Habits of the Heart*, 35.

[22] Cassidy, "Me Media," 56.

conformist in our nonconformity, and the market economy thrives. Although we all might dress differently, we all haunt the same mall. Presumably a single factory could produce enough cell phones for all of us if it only had to produce one kind of cell phone. But the variations in style and features are what keep the designers, the advertisers, and the factory workers employed.

Of course, expressing our individuality isn't all about consumption. After graduating from college, I spent nine months wandering around Central America trying to "find myself" so that I would know what I was supposed to be expressing. I hadn't yet heard a friend's warning that she found herself "and it was awful." I spent many an afternoon in the cafés of Guatemala musing on how to cultivate and express myself and on how to explore my "vast cosmic identities." The tradition taught to me by Western books, movies, and music was deep within me, and I was trying to do my duty in relation to it. In the end, though, I had at least a small sense that I wasn't going to be an Asher Lev. My "scream" was not so penetratingly unique and wonderful that I could sell it to others. Mostly, I would be doomed to buy the better-drawn screams of others.

And I longed for something better. At the time I knew of a small group of people living in Christian community in San Francisco called the Church of the Sojourners. An important passage for them was and is Ephesians 4, especially v. 13, which speaks of all of us growing into the full stature of Christ. Their idea was and is that our highest calling is not so much to express who we are but to express who Christ is. Interestingly, Ephesians 4:13 appears in the context of everyone using their gifts to build up the body. Individuality is not suppressed, but it is valued as contributing to the growth of the body. Only as each member performs his or her unique function is the body built up.

During my first year at Sojourners, I felt emotions that were hard to name churning in my guts. When I tried to figure out what I was feeling, I could only identify a vague sense of betraying myself and a sense of guilt for becoming part of a "collective." It seemed like a failure of courage or perhaps of responsibility on my part. Then I came across Bellah's book *Habits of the Heart,* and I was then able to pull out the tangle of emotions, name them, and begin to unknot them. My guts had been knotted in a struggle between the tradition of expressive individualism and the biblical tradition of holy community. Naming what was going on inside me helped me take some initial steps toward being more obedient to the biblical tradition than to my Western culture.

I suspect that most of us need this clarity. If we attempt to live within the Christian tradition yet to buy the contemporary commitment to expressive individualism, our lives will be the alienated struggle of Asher Lev. We must become clear that our deepest calling is to express who God is and to be together with others, Christ's body on earth. Without clarity on this point, I fear we might repeat what happened during the 1960s. During that era, when the times were "a changin'," many people dropped out of mainstream culture and joined communes. But not many of those communities lasted. For many, joining a commune was more a commitment to expressing an identity different from the mainstream than a commitment to living as God's holy people. The ultimate commitment to self made a deep unity with others impossible. So the very thing that gave rise to community killed it.

Reflection on this history leads me to ask, how might communities of obedience be formed that last, communities that do not oppress and violate the self, communities that joyfully incorporate the self into the holy body of Christ?

The Role of the Rule

Readers of St. Benedict's rule may become engrossed in the practical instructions that Benedict makes for a life together. Helpful as these instructions are, the written rule itself holds an importance and power we should be careful not to overlook. For 1500 years the Rule of St. Benedict has sustained Christian communities in a remarkably healthy and vital way.

Because of our Western history, living one's life under a "rule" probably doesn't seem very attractive to most of us. It may seem antithetical to spontaneity, individuality, and freedom. But again, opposing the rule to a life of freedom sets up a false choice. There is no real way to live without a rule. If we say that we value spontaneity, individuality, and freedom, then that is our rule, albeit a kind of informal, unwritten rule. Each of us could be said to have our own personal unwritten rule. Usually it is an amalgam of messages from our culture and parents and peers about how and how much we should work, consume, relax, procreate, exercise, eat, worship, commute, sleep, and the like. St. Benedict's rule is a bold and imaginative stab at what it might mean to live the best life possible—a life in which we truly live out our purpose as human beings.

Having a written rule allows us to think practically about what it might mean to live out a holy life day by day and hour by hour. Like a yardstick, it allows us to think about how our lives actually compare to a conception of what it might mean to live a life completely devoted to God.

A written rule helps to distinguish between what is essential and what is peripheral. The story is told of one community in which newcomers were protesting that there were too many unwritten rules. Newcomers explained that they were constantly feeling judged by numerous unspoken expectations about how to eat and dress and recreate. The community undertook the task of writing down all the unwritten expectations and eventually came up with something like twelve pages of single spaced unwritten rules. In the end, that exercise helped the community distinguish between what was essential to their vision and to allow for more diversity in nonessentials.

A written rule might also help us to be in dialogue with both our Christian tradition and our contemporaries. If a community decides to adopt a way of life or a rule other than St. Benedict's, it might be helpful to compare that rule to the *Rule of St. Benedict*. Is the community's life a serious attempt at a holy life, or is it a mere veneer of spirituality on what is essentially a modern, worldly life? A written rule can also be a foundation for dialogue with other Christians. For a while, the Church of the Sojourners had an unofficial rule of life posted on its website. We were surprised to find that one mission organization was passing it out to all its members as a way of thinking about a life with kingdom priorities. This sharing of the unofficial rule led to many good and sometimes challenging conversations with those missionaries, about everything from dating to economic sharing.

For those of us raised in the free-church Biblicist tradition, the question might be asked, "Why have a rule at all? Isn't the Bible a good enough guide?" It is in fact the Bible that provides the model for coming up with concrete practices in various cultural situations.

The book of Leviticus, for example, provides an extensive "rule" for an agrarian, tribal society surrounded by kingdoms worshipping other gods. It served to distinguish Israel from the surrounding tribes and provided a way of seeing the most daily tasks as part of living as God's people. The New Testament, too, prescribes certain practices that were meant for the church in specific cultural situations. In 1 Corinthians, Paul gives instructions about eating meat sacrificed to idols, about head coverings, about celebrating the Lord's Supper, and about orderly worship. Trying to apply all of those instructions directly to our churches today would be odd and often unhelpful. But we understand Paul's project. Paul is trying to come up with concrete ways that Christians might live out the way of Jesus in their time and culture. Paul wants the Christians of his time to live as a holy people who are a light to those around them.

So, too, in our time and culture, it is worth thinking about concrete and particular ways to live out the way of Jesus. As it is, the lives of many Christians look more like the lives of the pagans around us rather than like the lives of a people characterized by the self-sacrificing love, generosity, and faithfulness of Jesus. Jesus talked so much about money and power and mercy. And yet, how do our lives differ remarkably from others' in our handling of money and power and mercy? Having a rule might help us think about concrete practices to resist the default rule of our time. We might commit to living on a certain amount of money and giving the rest away, to praying daily with others, to not having a TV, or to giving to everyone who asks.

Of course there are dangers in having a rule. Having a rule puts us at serious risk of becoming legalistic or of falling into self-righteousness. We must avidly guard against those twin beasts by always remembering that the rule is not the goal. God is the goal. A rule is a tool. It simply helps us give ourselves to God. People who are actually getting closer to the holy God have a growing sense of their own sinfulness and inability, and that the entire process of drawing near to God is enabled by grace. If the rule moves us toward legalism or a sense of superiority, then we have mistaken the means for the end.

Living in obedience to a rule is a way of taking what we learn from Scripture and tradition and from turning that wisdom into daily graces that make, fit, and feed our bodies and our hearts. In the ancient poem of Hafiz titled "Let's Eat," Hafiz asks what we are waiting for. All people are hungry for God; we all want to feast at God's table. Hafiz urges us to get on with the eating. Living by a rule is one way of finding and enjoying God's feast.[23]

Characteristics of Community Leaders

Many communities are started by a charismatic person. One possible role of a rule is to focus the community more on a shared vision for a common life rather than on the charisma of one person. A rule also gives the community stability if the founding member dies or leaves. At the same time, Ephesians 4 depicts Jesus Christ going to great lengths to give the church gifted leaders. It says,

> The gifts he gave were that some would be apostles, some prophets, some evangelists, some pastors and teachers, to equip the saints for the work of ministry, for building up the body of Christ, until all of us come to the unity of the faith and of the knowledge of the Son of God, to maturity, to the measure of the full stature of Christ. (Eph 4:11–13)

What wisdom can we glean from Scripture and from St. Benedict to know how to receive these leaders? How can we discern whether they are people worthy to be obeyed?

As Ephesians indicates, leaders are not only gifted; they use their gifts for the building up of the church. Gifts are not for the sake of their egos or to construct a monument of community to themselves; gifts are given to create a holy people who resemble Christ. St. Benedict makes this similar point by saying that the abbot should "not command, teach, or demand anything contrary to the way of the Lord" (RB 2).[24] Benedict goes on to describe parental characteristics of the abbot: the abbot should be just, caring and diligent. He should model goodness more through his life than through his words. He ought to love all equally and "mix encouragement with reproof" (RB 2).[25]

At its worst, Benedict's "paternalism" might conjure up images of smug and authoritarian males who believe that "father knows best," images of a condescending superiority that stifles and subju-

[23] Hafiz. "Let's Eat," 22.
[24] Meisel and del Maestro, *Rule of St. Benedict*, 48.
[25] Ibid., 48–49.

gates others under the "alpha male." As the rule makes clear, however, abbots are to be chosen based on their obedience to God and to the rule. Such people have made real strides in dying to self and are more likely to be wise and humble rather than controlling and authoritarian. Still, for modern people another image might be helpful. John Alexander suggested that we at Sojourners discern who had "mother" hearts, and that we make such people our leaders.

MOTHER LOVE

Living at Sojourners, I've had the chance to watch some outstanding mothers. They get up at night, in spite of being bone-tired, to nourish their newborns; they pat their babies comfortingly on the back until they get spit upon; they put up with pouts and tantrums and still make dinner for the little culprits. They discipline their kids, but I get the sense that the discipline is almost always for the children's sake rather than out of frustration or out of an agenda for control. The mothers I know seem to have time and energy for their kids that I can't imagine. And they take a deep delight in their kids. Happily enough, I've seen these traits in the men at Sojourners as well as in the women.

I think most of us respond well to (and know that we need) that kind of love. One of the simplest graces I experienced on coming to Sojourners was that wise and good elders had a "mother love" for me. These people weren't consumed by their jobs or hobbies or recreation. They had carefully made time in their lives to care for others. They had made their lives to be about their "kids." We visited prisoners together, we drank beers together, we vacationed together, we argued together, and we cooked dinner together. Life overlapped enough, and they cared enough. Being a good leader was almost that simple. And that difficult.

LISTENING

Another "motherlike" characteristic I noticed in the leaders I first knew at Church of the Sojourners was their capacity to listen. As they listened to me, I sensed they were listening both to me and beyond me. Their deepest desire was to hear God. When I spoke to them about a problem or a bad day, they listened intently. They listened not mostly to communicate empathy or to formulate a wise solution to my problem but rather as a way of hearing what God was up to in me. In response to me, they would often wonder about what God was saying or doing in that circumstance. Their constant redirection of me and of others toward God is perhaps another way they exercised leadership and a reason that they had been named leaders.

St. Benedict counsels that the abbot listen to the youngest member of the community when the community is to make an important decision, because it is never known through whom God will speak. Community leaders listen for the voice of God as a mother might listen for her child. They listen for God's voice whenever, however, and from whomever it comes. Their concern is not so much their own wisdom or intuition or reputation but the voice of God and how that voice might lead.

As a recipient of listening, motherlike love, I responded to that love by being obedient to it. I took copious notes on those leaders' sermons and talks. I tried to read the Bible as they did. I confessed my deepest sins to them and to God, and I sought them out to mentor me. I asked them how to pray and worship and love. In spite of my sense of entitlement, I tried to imitate them by living more simply and by loving the poor in ways that weren't just about making me feel good about myself. Because of those leaders' good teaching and example, I began to realize that what I wanted was not so much to express myself as to be part of Jesus's body in this world.

Shared Leadership

As I grew in my desire to be part of Christ's body, I began to see more clearly the importance of mutual submission. Yes, I had a gift or two to offer, but I could only offer if others were willing to follow my lead. And in this realization, I began to understand more deeply my need to follow others' lead. If I try to lead others in worship, my leadership only works as well as the others who give themselves to singing and prayer and praise. And then as someone else tries to teach, that teaching only takes effect in my life as I listen diligently, grapple with it, and try to apply it. According to Ephesians 4, the head of the body is Christ. All the rest of us are body parts, who need to obey the head and mutually submit to one another.

I once met a young person who was and is a very good preacher. He came to live at Sojourners, and I was excited to have him as part of the preaching and teaching team. One of the pastors, however, advised against recruiting him for the preaching and teaching team. That pastor knew that this newer person most needed a year of sabbath and freedom from church responsibilities. I found this advice puzzling, but knowing the advisor's gifts, I submitted to his wisdom. In retrospect, I'm sure that the pastor was right with his advice, and that allowing the preacher a time of sabbath was by far the best way of loving him.

Through experiences such as the preacher's sabbath, we have learned the importance of shared leadership. Although Sojourners is a small church community, we are big on teams. We have a teaching and preaching team, an oversight team, a pastoral team, and many worship teams. We've come to realize that no one person is omnicompetent, and that expecting any one person to have all or most spiritual gifts puts undue pressure on that person and makes other parts of the body wither.

Expanding Alasdair MacIntyre's statement that we need a new St. Benedict, Jon Stock has commented that what we really need are new Benedictines.[26] I take this to mean that what are not needed are more people to start and lead new Christian communities that will "get it right." Rather, what are needed are humble Christians who are willing to live in mutual submission with one another. We need Christians who can be obedient to the gifts of others and enthusiastically offer whatever gifts they might possess.

By God's grace, such people might form truly healthy communities that act as the body of Christ. I once remember reading in a college physiology text that at every moment, our bodies are producing cancer cells. At any given time, there are mutated cells in our bodies—cells that have the potential to multiply into useless, aggressive, invasive cells and to ultimately cause our death. But, moment by moment, our immune system searches for these cancerous cells, captures them, and destroys them. I suspect that just as the human body hosts potentially deadly cells, so our communities may include those born with the will to power and with arrogance, and facing the temptation to coerce; these qualities would make us bad

[26] Jon Stock, e-mail message to author, July 23, 2006.

and dangerous leaders. But healthy bodies have a way of recognizing such dangers and, with the help and grace of God, of guarding against abuses of authority. The solution is not to give up submitting to the gifts of others, as the Enlightenment tradition might teach us. Rather, in the language of Ephesians 4:15–16, we must strive to form a body in which each part is "working properly" to "promote" the body's growth, so that we can grow "in every way into him who is the head, into Christ."

At one time in my life, I remember finding it difficult to acknowledge others' gifts, let alone to submit to them. An obvious gift in another often produced envy and jealousy in me. Since I was busily trying to express and develop the "gift" within myself, it seemed to me that others' gifts, by comparison, diminished me and showed me up. As I've grown in a vision for Christ's body, I now often find myself rejoicing in others' gifts. In some sense, their gifts are "mine" because we are part of the same body. Because we are connected, I get to receive others' gifts and to offer them my own. South African theologian Allan Boesak once said, "the pinnacle of lovelessness is not our unwillingness to be a neighbor to someone, but our unwillingness to allow them to be a neighbor to us."[27] As I allow others to use their gifts for me, I find that I am a true neighbor, not just trying to bolster my own ego through a one-way "ministry" to others. Obedience as expressed in mutual submission to one another turns out to be a joyful exchange of gifts.

Community of Communities

In thinking about what promotes community in which a real and healthy obedience is possible, the last but vitally important element is that communities to be connected to other communities. For St. Benedict, operating within the care of the Catholic Church, it was possible to take unresolved community problems to church leaders outside the community.

Many of us who are Protestants are realizing our deep need for community; the next step is that we realize the need of our communities for the larger church. This book is an attempt to learn from the church of the past by mining the wisdom of St. Benedict's Rule.

[27] Boesak, *Farewell to Innocence*, 5.

Along with the wisdom of the Christian past, however, we also need relationships with the larger church in the present.

About twelve years ago, the Church of the Sojourners came across an affiliation of church communities called Shalom Mission Communities (SMC). We tried hard to have real relationships with them. We invested in plane tickets to visit them, made regular phone calls, went on retreats with them, and even had some marriages result from the contact. We also began a practice that we called "accountability visits." Every three years or so, members of the Shalom Mission Communities would come to Sojourners and interview each of the Sojourner members. The "accountability board" then gave a report and recommendations to the entire congregation. This seemed like a good practice, something like getting a periodic physical checkup.

Then, in two years' time, two of the primary pastors at Sojourners both died of cancer. The community went through a hard process of grieving and of questioning God. There were those of us who wondered if we should call it quits as a community. During that time, we called upon SMC to come and visit. Because of our history of relationship and accountability, they already knew us well and were able to come alongside us and encourage us in vital ways that helped us to keep going.

Months after that visit, a major conflict arose between two of the three members on our oversight team. The conflict dragged on for months and made life even harder for the whole community, at an already difficult time. Again, we called on SMC to send help. The SMC members suggested a course of action, and within weeks the conflict was over, and a real reconciliation had taken place. Connection with other communities proved essential for our health and perspective. I suspect that Sojourners would do well to become part of a denomination (and some of us wonder if we should become Catholics). The point is that as communities maintain connection with the larger church, they will be healthier places, where positive obedience is possible.

Orphans

Reflecting on my attempts to be obedient, after seventeen years of life in community I confess that I still find the word *obedience* to be less than warm and inviting. I've tried to reflect on the reasons for my limited of enthusiasm about the word *obedience*. And as I've tried to explain here, I think the Enlightenment tradition has given the idea of obedience a lot of bad press, and much of that bad propaganda still lives on in me, and in us as Westerners. I also believe the Bible's witness that I am and we are rebels at heart, and because of our rebellious hearts, I doubt that many of us will manage to love the word *obedience*. I've also had my doubts about what God asks us to be obedient to. I've had my doubts about Scripture and about a Christian tradition that seems such a crazy history of theological wrangling and historical accident. And living so close to the leaders of the community of which I'm a part, I have found it easy to see the sins and flaws in them.

But if I could live life all over again, I would choose to be more obedient rather than less. Or to say it a little more precisely, I would choose to be more obedient to Scripture, to the Christian tradition, and to godly people rather than to the other things I've been obedient to. I recently heard it said of someone that "he gave up on becoming a masterpiece in order to be part of The Masterpiece." I wish that could be said of me. Romans 6:16–17 speaks of us as being either slaves of sin or obedient to righteousness. Being a slave to sin makes life truly "rough." Being obedient to righteousness, on the other hand, is, I imagine, like a bird discovering its wings. Righteousness is what we were made for.

A hauntingly beautiful song is Gillian Welch's "Orphan Girl." The singer laments that, whereas she has had friendships, she has not known family ties. I sense that this song resonates deeply with many modern people because we've been parented by a tradition that turns us into abandoned children at an early age. At its worst, our Western tradition teaches us that the older generation wants us to mindlessly conform, that the Christian tradition is oppressive, and that the best we can do is to run away and follow our individual hearts. Wandering in search of our hearts, we are accosted by strangers offering us candy in the form of commoditized goods, styles, and services, so that we can express ourselves. We meet other wandering children along the way and call them friends, but we sense the loss of a deep rootedness in a true family. We know that we're far from home.

As the song continues, I find intriguing Welch's line "but when he calls me I will be able." Does it mean that someday Jesus will just grab our hand and haul us into heaven to meet our true family? In Ezekiel 36:24–28, God sees all God's wandering children and promises to give them hearts of flesh rather than stone (v. 26). The next verses explain that this new heart will be capable of obedience, and therefore God's children will be able to live as God's family, and God as their God. "I will put my spirit within you, and make you follow my statutes and be careful to observe my ordinances. Then you shall live in the land that I gave to your ancestors; and you shall be my people, and I will be your God" (vv. 27–28). Happily, it seems that there is a chance to live as God's family even now.

As Augustine realized so long ago, our hearts are restless orphans until we find our rest in our true home—God (*Conf.* 1.1.1). St. Benedict, building on Augustine's insight, drew out a map to that home, a map that he called a rule. This map shows that the way to God is the road of obedience. If we are willing and able to follow that good map, we will, I believe, find ourselves walking with family toward home.

4

Stability

Jon Stock

The idea of making a vow of stability, of taking a vow to stay in one place or to live under one rule for the rest of your life, is offensive to most ears. Our culture places such a premium on freedom of choice and freedom to keep options open that we have lost the imagination to see ways that a vow of stability might be a good thing.

I should admit that while I am not Benedictine, I have lived under a vow of stability for almost twenty years. I have not always found this vow convenient, but I can call it good. Each September, I gather with my brothers and sisters for a weekend retreat, and we reaffirm our Statement of Commitment. So I am quite biased in favor of stability. Much of what I consider good and rich about life in community has its roots in our vow of stability.

What I intend to do in this essay is first to examine the Benedictine vow of stability and then to move to biblical texts that encourage stability. The argument from Scripture will refine the concepts of *ḥesed* and *agapē* introduced in the discussion of the legitimacy of vows. Finally, I will speak specifically about the vow of stability and about its consequences within Church of the Servant King, the community of which I am a part.

Benedict of Nursia

The vow of stability is central to Benedictine life and practice. At the close of the prologue to the Rule of St. Benedict, we read:

> We are, therefore, about to found a school of the Lord's service, in which we hope to introduce nothing harsh or burdensome. But even if, to correct vices or to preserve charity, sound reason dictate[s] anything that turn[s] out somewhat stringent, do not at once fly in dismay from the way of salvation, the beginning of which cannot but be narrow. But as we advance in the religious life and faith, we shall run

the way of God's commandments with expanded hearts and unspeakable sweetness of love; so that never departing from His guidance and persevering in the monastery in His doctrine till death, we may by patience share in the sufferings of Christ, and be found worthy to be coheirs with Him of His kingdom. (RB P)[1]

Chapter 58 of the Rule of St. Benedict, "Of the manner of admitting brethren" puts forth the following:

Now this is the manner of his reception. In the oratory, in the presence of all, he shall pronounce stability . . . and this before God and his saints, so that he may know that should he ever act in opposition he will be condemned by him whom he mocks. . . . Let him understand . . . that he is no longer free to leave the monastery or to withdraw his neck from under the yoke of the rule . . . knowing that henceforward he will not have the disposition of even his own body. (RB 58)[2]

By the vow of stability, the monk promises to stay put in one place for life and to find God in that place and with those particular people. The monk's physical commitment to a particular monastery is linked with his spiritual stability. He cannot have one kind of stability without the other. Benedict contrasts the rootedness of the community-based monks with those monastic mavericks he calls "gyrovagues" (translated in what follows as "landlopers").

But the fourth class of monks is that called Landlopers, who keep going their whole life long from one province to another, staying three or four days at a time in different cells as guests. Always roving and never settled, they indulge their passions and the cravings of their appetite, and are in every way worse than the Sarabaites [those who live without an abbot]. It is better to pass all these over in silence than to speak of their most wretched life.[3]

Benedict has no patience for "church shoppers."

---

[1] Verheyen, *Holy Rule*, http://www.monachos.net/monasticism/benedict/rule.shtml

[2] Wolter *Principles*, 43.

[3] Verheyen, *Holy Rule*.

Benedict's rule presumes and intends that members of the monastery are a family and that the vow of stability is a natural consequence of their desire to live as God's new family. Benedict understood that a monastery is not just a group of individuals who happen to have found their way to a particular place. For Benedict, those individuals have been called by God to form together into a particular type of community. This community is best understood as a family that shares a common likeness—the likeness of their Father.

> This membership in a family which is essentially supernatural but which nevertheless has an attractive naturalness about it, is the consequence of the Benedictine vow of stability. From it flow the precious filial virtues of a strong attachment to the monastery of one's profession, a readiness to cooperate faithfully in the work in which the community is engaged and a love for one's confreres which dispenses with flattery and sentimentality but is prepared unselfishly to sacrifice personal desires and interests in favor of those of the monastic family and of one's brother in Christ. Because Benedict values the family spirit so highly, for major infractions of the Rule he imposes temporary exclusion of the monk from the life of the family as an especially severe penalty.[4]

This language of family is essential to understanding the logic of stability. Just as healthy biological families end up tied to one another for life, so it is for God's new family. Once one truly has been grafted into this new family of God, it is inconceivable to think that such ties could merely be given up without much consequence.

The Benedictine tradition also sees stability of location as essential to the development of this family of God. Michael Casey, in his fine essay on stability, comments:

> this is not to say that the primary object of the vow is enclosure, as this is envisaged canonically. It does mean, however, that the reality of stability cannot be realized without spending a substantial part of one's life and investing one's energies within monastery limits . . . When presence in the community falls below a critical point, a sense of belonging evaporates.[5]

[4] Hunkeler, *It Began with Benedict*, 46.
[5] Casey, *Unexciting Life*, 241.

Without a place to gather and live, there can only be a simulacrum of family. Without a place where shoulders are rubbed, chores are shared, and songs are sung, we are denied the type of real living necessary for spiritual growth.

The Cistercians of the Strict Observance[6] state the following with regard to the vow of stability: "By the vow of stability within his community a brother obliges himself there to make constant use of the means of the spiritual craft, trusting in the providence of God who has called him to this place and to this group of brothers."[7] Within this family of God, stability provides the monastic with a foundation from which to continue on in the spiritual craft. The popular vision of spirituality in the West often takes a gnostic form that renders corporality and the "other" irrelevant. Benedictine monasticism rejects this form of spirituality, finding that it is in the committed, embodied encounter with others that we often find the framework for spiritual growth. Many see monastic life as an escape from the world; the monk, on the other hand, sees it as a way of life that brings one into sustained confrontation with realties that might otherwise be avoided, disguised or denied. Those outside of monastic practice are often quick to write off monastic experience as a flight from humanity, whereas the monk understands that they are having the most human of experiences within the walls of the monastery— that of personal intercommunion. Casey states that

> part of the bonding of a monastic community results from
> the common exposure to the ultimate demands of existence,
> the frailty of their response, and working of grace negating
> their weakness. To experience communion at such a pro-
> found level needs the security of lifelong commitment, not

---

[6] Cistercians were a Benedictine reform primarily driven by Stephen Harding (d. 1134), who was soon joined by Bernard of Clairvaux (1090–1153). The Cistercian reform was a return to the literal observance of the *Rule of St. Benedict*. Cistercians of the Strict Observance, also known as Trappists, are a later reform initiated in 1664 at the Abbey of Notre Dame de la Grande Trappe, in reaction to the relaxation of practices in many Cistercian monasteries. Like the earlier reform, the Trappist attempt is guided by the *Rule of St. Benedict*.

[7] *Constitutions and Statutes*, chapter 1, C. 9. http://www.ocso.org/cst-stat/cc-m-en.htm.

only to God, not only to the monastic idea, but also to the people with whom the journey is made.[8]

Such a vision incorporates the Johannine understanding, which ties our love of God to our love for our brothers and sisters. It is also the case, as Bonhoeffer points out,[9] that mere ideals are easily corrupted when they are divorced from the truth of God and from real human relations. Stability ought to tie us to all three: to God, to the ideal, and to one another—for the duration.

When such stability is in place, then we have availed ourselves to the means of the spiritual craft. For it is now, as Casey points out,

> when external circumstances are relatively unchanging, we are more frequently confronted with those elements in our being that need reformation. . . . Aspects of the self that could be successfully concealed in looser association assert themselves in a close community and cause pain—to others, certainly, but more especially to ourselves. Stability protects this process of purgation. We are tied down under the surgeon's knife. . . . For all of us, much of the challenge of stability is the interior task of learning to sit with our own impairment, allowing ourselves to be hollowed out as the frontiers of dread expand, blaming neither ourselves nor others, but bearing the weight of sin, absorbing its malice and not allowing ourselves the luxury of wilting under the pressure or passing the time devising means of evading the truth.[10]

Ultimately, stability is a matter of learning to love. Casey cites Anselm's *Letter 37*, which speaks of setting down "roots of love."[11] Anselm understands that we will always find reasons to be unhappy where we are. We will always be able to find people who irritate us. We will always find ways to grow weary in the face of the daily grind. It is only when we learn to love those that we are close to that our perceptions begin to change, and such love cannot be nurtured without the constancy of stability. Stability and love feed off

[8] Casey, *Unexciting Life*, 240–41.
[9] Bonhoeffer, *Life Together*, 35–37.
[10] Casey, *Unexciting Life*, 243–44.
[11] Ibid., 245–46.

each other. Conversely, one without the other becomes some sort of parody. Stability without love gives birth to all forms of dysfunction—legalism, cannibalism, or the development of a mere husk of a community driven daily by an established bureaucracy but failing to produce an actual heartbeat. Love without stability, on the other hand, permeates our popular culture. It is an insatiable love that is driven by a consumerist spirituality that, like a vampire, selfishly consumes the other and moves on in search of further consumption. Such love is marked by its self-centered shallowness and is merely a shadow of *agapē*. Monastic spirituality forces us to face up to the truth that if we are to grow in *agapē*, we must give ourselves to stability. Casey states:

> to live monastic profession as a Cistercian, is to be a lifelong learner in the school of love. Stability is an important factor in this development and, on the other hand, without genuine love stability is meaningless.[12]

The Benedictine vow of stability is prophetic in our age of consumerism, restlessness, and frenzy. Americans are wandering souls in search of a self, bouncing from one answer to the next, never willing to stay in one place if stability might mean the retardation of fulfilled desire. From an early age, we are taught to think with our belly. If our current place does not immediately fulfill our appetites and felt needs, then we go shopping. By this vow of stability, Benedict brought transience and mobility—which he believed to be the tangible expressions of human pride, independence and self-will—under the healing influence of obedience. Our immediate impulse when strife and contention arise is often to run, to avoid resolution for the sake of preserving pride and nursing resentment. In a day when people flow in and out of churches, imagine the effect that stability could have on our ability to love one another, to bear one another's burdens, to resolve conflicts, and to forgive each other. Benedictine spirituality and practices arise from an understanding that if we hope to form communities that bear witness to Yahweh, we must stay together. In many cases, we are only able to discern how it is that we should live together by committing to stay together in the first place. For it is only by sticking it out through the happy and the sad, the

---

[12] Ibid., 253.

comedic and the tragic, that we learn fully what God's community of *shalom* might begin to look like. Benedict considered the vow of stability as essential to the training of the soul.

We'll turn now to consider biblical testimony to stability, tracing both themes and narratives in the Old and New Testaments.

Ruth

A most poignant example of stability in Scripture is Ruth the Moabite. She declares to her mother-in-law Naomi:

> Do not press me to leave you or to turn back from following you! Where you go, I will go; where you lodge, I will lodge; your people shall be my people and your God my God. Where you die, I will die—there will I be buried. May the Lord do thus and so to me, and more as well, if even death parts me from you! (Ruth 1:16–17)

The story of Ruth is familiar to most of us. Elimelech takes Naomi and their two sons to Moab during a famine in Judah. They settle in the land, and their sons take Moabite wives, Orpah and Ruth. In time, all of three men die, leaving the women to consider their options. Naomi decides to return to her clan in Judah; bitter and with few options, she tells the other women to return to their mother's house. Orpah kisses her mother-in-law and returns to her family, but Ruth clings to Naomi reciting the stunning passage above. With the death of the men in this agrarian culture, Ruth, Naomi, and Orpah's socioeconomic framework collapses. The women are left empty and with no standing in society. Orpah sensibly rejoins her Moabite family, but Ruth chooses, against all reason, the scarcity of Naomi. Ruth's is a decision of great consequence; Naomi and her Moabite daughter-in-law travel to Bethlehem. Moabites are not welcome in Judah:

> No Ammonite or Moabite shall be admitted to the assembly of the Lord. Even to the tenth generation, none of their descendants shall be admitted to the assembly of the Lord, because they did not meet you with food and water on your journey out of Egypt, and because they hired against you Balaam son of Beor, from Pethor of Mesopotamia, to curse you. (Deut 23: 3–4)

We must keep in mind what Ruth, the Moabite, represents to Israel. Aside from the account of the inhospitality of her people in the plains of Moab, recounted in Numbers, Moabites represent the sin of incest to Israel, personified by the daughters of Lot who bear Ammon and Moab (Gen 19:31–38).[13] This is the social environment that Ruth willingly walks into as a result of her loyalty to Naomi.

Upon the women's reaching Bethlehem at the beginning of the barley harvest, Ruth asks Naomi to let her go into the field and glean behind the reapers (Ruth 2:2). As Ruth comes to the part of the field belonging to Naomi's kinsman, Boaz, Boaz asks: "To whom does this young woman belong?" (Ruth 2:5). When it becomes clear to Boaz that this is the Moabite who came back with Naomi, he responds to Ruth unexpectedly, graciously offering her not only the right to glean but also a share in their water and protection from the young men (Ruth 2:8–10). When Ruth asks him, "Why have I found favor in your sight?" (2:10), Boaz reveals that he is fully aware of all that Ruth has done for her mother-in-law and blesses Ruth, saying, "may the Lord reward you for your deeds and may you have a full reward from the Lord, the God of Israel, under whose wings you have come for refuge" (Ruth 2:12). At mealtime, Ruth is invited to share in bread and wine. Boaz heaps up for her parched grain and, again, instructs the young men to leave her alone (Ruth 2:14–16). This gracious gleaning arrangement continues until the end of the barley and wheat harvests (Ruth 2:23).

If, as several commentators suggest, Ruth is postexilic and most likely contemporary with the books of Ezra and Nehemiah, then the generosity of Boaz is extraordinary in light of the cultural pressure to exclude foreign women (Ezra 9:1–15; Nehemiah 13:1). By inviting Ruth into the field and integrating her among his young women, Boaz is beginning the incorporation of the Moabite woman into Israel. Why? Because of Ruth's *ḥesed*, which transcends law and custom.

At the end of the gleaning season, Naomi sends Ruth to Boaz at the threshing floor, so that Ruth might find some security: "Wash and anoint yourself, and put on your best clothes but do not make yourself known to the man until he has finished eating and drink-

---

[13] For a broader discussion of this element see LaCocque, *Ruth*, 21–28. LaCocque makes significant uses of Fishbane, *Biblical Interpretation*, 115–20.

ing. When he lies down, observe the place where he lies; then, go and uncover his feet and lie down; and he will tell you what to do." Ruth's response is characteristic: "All that you tell me I will do." (Ruth 3:3–5). So Ruth does approach Boaz and places herself at his feet, inviting him, upon his waking, to "spread your cloak over your servant" (Ruth 3:9).

Boaz's response is one of blessing: "May you be blessed by the Lord my daughter; this last instance of your loyalty [*hesed*] is better than the first; you have not gone after young men, whether poor or rich. And now, my daughter, do not be afraid, I will do for you all that you ask . . ." (Ruth 3:10–11).

Boaz understands that Ruth is under no obligation to marry within Naomi's clan; she likely has younger, more vital options. But because Ruth has vowed stability to Naomi, Ruth has accepted the consequence of lying with Boaz on the threshing floor. In doing so, Ruth is assuring Naomi's future and the future of Elimelech's line as well as her own security. *Hesed* provokes *hesed*. Ruth's own loyalty to Naomi provokes a reciprocal response in Boaz, who clearly understands that here, on the threshing floor, this last instance of loyalty is better than the first. In offering to do whatever Ruth asks, Boaz in essence agrees to provide an heir for Naomi. Ruth has allowed a criterion other than romance to determine her actions; she is moved by her commitment to Naomi.

Boaz is not the closest next of kin; there is a kinsman more closely related to Ruth and Naomi. Someone else had the right to redeem. His name is not given. Boaz calls him "friend" in the NRSV (Ruth 4:1), but LaCocque translates this word "So-and-so" and assumes its meaning is pejorative.[14] What follows is a chapter that is dense with regard to the practice of the law (leading the conversation beyond the pale of our topic), a chapter in which Boaz reveals himself to be one who is well prepared for this discussion at the gates of Bethlehem. Boaz may not be a scribe, but he shows himself as one who understands the nuances of the law. The end result is that "So-and-so" evades his duty and gives up his claim as redeemer to Boaz. Taking on Ruth as a concubine would have been a viable option for "So-and-so," but to take Ruth as a concubine would have

---

[14] LaCocque, *Ruth*, 127.

complicated issues of lineage and inheritance. To "So-and-so," Ruth's redemption is not worth such a risk.

It is worth noting that Boaz, as redeemer of Naomi and Ruth, has no legal obligation to marry Ruth. Ruth might legally have become a mere concubine; but if Ruth had become only his concubine, Boaz would have failed to produce a legal heir for Naomi. Like Ruth's *ḥesed*, the *ḥesed* of Boaz transcends legal obligation and moves into the realm of generous excess. In a sense, Ruth's earlier act of *ḥesed*, in which she acts to reveal her willingness to extend Elimelech's line by proxy, provides an opportunity for Boaz to reciprocate, thus providing a whole knew future for Naomi, Ruth, and Boaz together. The story closes with the very strong suggestion that this *ḥesed* opens up a whole new future for Israel as well.

Genealogies are too often overlooked in the casual or devotional reading of Scripture. In the case of the book of Ruth, the genealogy makes an essential point.

> ". . . may your house be like to house of Perez, whom Tamar bore to Judah." So Boaz took Ruth and she became his wife. When they came together, the Lord made her conceive, and she bore a son.
>
> Then the women said to Naomi, "Blessed be the Lord, who has not left you this day without one with the right to redeem; and may his name be renowned in Israel! He shall be to you a restorer of life and a nourisher of your old age; for your daughter-in-law who loves you, who is more to you than seven sons, has borne him."
>
> Then Naomi took the child and laid him in her bosom, and became his nurse. The women of the neighborhood gave him a name, saying, "A son has been born to Naomi." They named him Obed; he became the father of Jesse, the father of David.
>
> Now these are the descendants of Perez: Perez became the father of Hezron, Hezron of Ram, Ram of Amminadab, Amminadab of Nahshon, Nahshon of Salmon, Salmon of Boaz, Boaz of Obed, Obed of Jesse, and Jesse of David. (Ruth 4:12–22)

Tamar was the daughter-in-law of Judah. She was the Canaanite wife of Er and was long a widow because Er's brother Onan refused to marry her, and Judah withheld from Tamar his third son, Shelah, past the promised time. So, out of desperation, Tamar offered herself disguised as a prostitute to Judah and bore his twins, Perez and Zerah (Genesis 38).[15] Boaz, a descendent of Perez, is the son of Rahab, the prostitute. The result of the union of Boaz with the Moabite Ruth is Obed, the grandfather of David. LaCocque claims that "[t]his is what the book of Ruth brings as tangible proof to the accuracy of the audacious interpretation of the Law by Boaz following the dazzling intuition of the Moabite."[16] The ultimate fruit of the stability of Ruth and the generous compassion of Boaz (their *ḥesed*) is David (of course, the New Testament genealogies lead us further—to Jesus of Nazareth).

> [T]he central thesis of Ruth is as follows: a foreigner, a Moabite, following the example of another foreigner, a Canaanite [Tamar], proves to be the opportune instrument of salvation history . . . The narrative repeats, in nobler terms, an older story, the conclusion of which had remained unresolved. Ruth brings Tamar's audacity to fruition while performing an act of similar audacity. Everything should logically (and morally) conclude in infamy; but to the contrary, this accumulation of extravagances is necessary for the birth of David-Messiah.[17]

The point is not that what was outside the law is now permissible, but that excessive acts of *ḥesed*, such as Ruth's vow of stability, transcend the law in their redemptive power.[18] Outrageous love can heal, or as the epistle exhorts, "Above all, maintain constant love for one another, for love covers a multitude of sins" (1 Pet 4:13).

Ironically, a vow of stability, which is considered by many Christians to be some sort of popish legalism, instead leads to freedom from hopeless legalism. What the book of Ruth reveals is that

---

[15] LaCocque, *Ruth*, 51, 139. LaCocque sees strong parallels between the book of Ruth and Genesis 38.

[16] Ibid., 149.

[17] Ibid.

[18] Ibid., 120. Here LaCocque notes, "In the economy of the Law, the adultery-incest-prostitution of Tamar remains what it is. Similarly, the enticement of Boaz by Ruth is an illustration of the feminine traps that the wisdom literature recommends running from (cf. Prov 5:1–20; 6:20—7:37). In the economy of *ḥesed*, on the other hand, these same acts are transformed, because they are acts of love and sacrifice."

Ruth's stability, her practice of *ḥesed*, helps to break down any idea that the law provides the only guidance to community issues. Stable loyalty can and will break down legalism. (Or legalism will break down loyalty.) The two cannot coexist for any extended period of time (though sometimes it may take years to realize this). In many ways Ruth is a radical and subversive book. A female who is also a Moabite brings redemption that transcends the law through her *ḥesed*. It is a story that disorients the religious reader and provides a path of reorientation. The message of Ruth is revolutionary because it orients readers toward solutions marked by *ḥesed* or, using New Testament language, we might say *agapē*.

> Love redeems everything. Then the impasses open up, the foreigner is no longer foreign, the widow no longer a widow, the sterile woman (or so considered) gives birth, the lost property is returned to the family or the clan, the interrupted story resumes its course and is crowned by the advent of "David." More profoundly, the Law is no longer a means of control and power (at times of manipulation), but the instrument of peace, reconciliation, and equality. All the legal categories are transcended by an interpretation according to an amplifying and nonrestrictive norm. This is the reason the book of Ruth reminds one of the hermeneutic of Jesus.[19]

All of this because a Moabite woman has said to Naomi, "where you go, I will go." *Ḥesed*, expressed in this instance as including stability, creates a whole new world filled with new possibility. We might even call this possibility the Messianic way, if we are to take seriously the genealogies. In light of all this, it is difficult not to conclude that stability as an expression of *ḥesed* or love plays an essential role in the divine economy.

The Land

Land implies stability, the laying down of roots. In general, in order for stability to happen, it needs a place. Walter Brueggemann notes that "[l]and is a central, if not *the central theme* of biblical faith."[20] Yet land is always both a promise and a problem for the wandering

---

[19] Ibid., 27.

[20] Brueggemann, *Land*, 3.

people of God. Brueggemann asserts that the "land for which Israel yearns and which it remembers is never unclaimed space but is always *a place with Yahweh*."[21] Scripture imagines the people of God dwelling with Yahweh, yet plenty of counter-images prevail describing homelessness. Maybe the best image for our purpose is that of the resident alien. We require a place, even if we are not home yet. Here we encounter the greatest ambiguity between Benedictine stability and scriptural accounts. Certainly, God promises to be with the Israelites always and to promise them a place, but God is clearly with them before they get to the land and is with them when they are exiled from the land. So what are we to make of the importance of land or place?

Land is a gift, but it is not the primary gift. Prior to land is the creation of the people of God. Hence, land does not guarantee the presence of God, nor does it guarantee that all is right with the people of God. In fact, land can become a temptation. Landedness can take God's people away from vulnerable openness to God and one another. Security in the land can lead to idolatry, sloth, and the desire to control the land as if it were one's own.

As Israel prepares to enter the Promised Land, Brueggemann claims, "the central question at the boundary is this: Can Israel live in the land without being seduced by gods, without the temptation of coveting having its way? Can Israel live in the land with all the precarious trust of landlessness?"[22] This is a relevant question for both old and new monasticism. Just as Cluny needed reformation in light of wealth created by its landedness, just as Church of the Servant King struggles not to be overwhelmed by growing affluence, so it was for Israel. Land is necessary, but it brings great temptation.

On the other hand, Brueggemann notes, "land is the means of Yahweh's word becoming full and powerful for Israel."[23] When land can be seen by the people of God as pure gift and as radical grace, then land is a blessing. Land is God's comfort to his people, to a people who is intended to become a comfort and blessing to the nations. Land becomes a place of hospitality, refuge, and worship. Land is necessary in order for God's people to fully embody their calling.

[21] Ibid., 5.

[22] Ibid, 59.

[23] Ibid., 48.

Land brings stability even while bringing danger and temptation to those who would practice stability in a place.

A close connection exists between covenant and land, and not only because the land is covenanted land (and, hence, gift). As may be surmised from my essay on vows, covenant and land are related by the stability they bring. Land is promised; God's promise is stable; Israel will be rooted in a stable place. Yet covenanted land is land with boundless possibilities, demands, and mysteries because covenanted land is land deeply connected with the covenanting God.

> Israel's involvement is always with land and with Yahweh, never only with Yahweh as though to live only in intense obedience, never only with land, as though simply to possess and manage; always *with land* and *with Yahweh*, always receiving gifts from land, always being addressed by Yahweh, always being assured and summoned, always being both nourished and claimed, always being of the family of earth, but always and at the same time Yahweh's peculiar listening partner in historical covenant.[24]

It may be that land is a blessing precisely because it confronts us with the ambiguous nature of our life together with God. Such a confrontation can save us from all sorts of nasty self-righteousness.

Jeremiah presents us with the truth that land can be both the place of idolatry and a place of renewal. For those who remain in the land, like Zedekiah, the land becomes a horror, yet for those who are sent of the exile we find blessing (Jer 24:4–7). As Brueggemann notes, here is "where the history of turf must find its next episode. Land is losable, and when lost newness comes."[25] Monastic history would seem to affirm this, as we see a decay of one place only to find renewal in another from Cluny, to Citeaux, to the Abbey of Notre Dame de la Grande Trappe. My own community has had similar experiences on a much smaller scale.

So, Yahweh tells the exiles,

> Build houses and live in them; plant gardens and eat their produce. Take wives and have sons and daughters; take wives for your sons, and give your daughters in marriage, that they

[24] Ibid., 52.
[25] Ibid., 124.

may bear sons and daughters; multiply there, and do not decrease. But seek the welfare of the city where I have sent you into exile, and pray to the Lord on its behalf, for in its welfare you will find your welfare. (Jer 29:5–7)

The exiles are to seek the *shalom* of the city; they are to settle down in Babylon for the long haul. As resident aliens, they are to infect the Babylonians with the politics of Yahweh, seeking the good of those who have defeated them (love your enemies!).

Yahweh calls his people to engage in the stability of place in the midst of exile, so that his way of living might take root. This is not to say that Yahweh has forgotten and moved on from Jerusalem, but it is to underscore how important place is to Yahweh—even in the midst of exile. In fact, Jeremiah's act of buying land in Judah (Jeremiah 32) is a complementary act of stability in the midst of trying times. All Yahweh's promises remain in place. "Just as I have brought all this great disaster on this people, so I will bring upon them all the good fortune that I now promise them. Fields shall be bought in the land of which you are saying. It is desolation" (Jer 32:42–43).

The ending of Jeremiah provokes even further consideration of the nature of the relationship between stability and land. Yahweh does have room for a remnant people in the land. "If you will only remain in this land, then I will build you up and not pull you down; I will plant you and not pluck you up; for I am sorry for the disaster that I have brought upon you" (Jer 42:10). But Johanan, a military commander, and the people do not trust the counsel of God. As has always been the temptation of the people of God, they choose to travel to Egypt rather than to remain in the land: "No, we will go to the land of Egypt, where we shall not see war, or hear the sound of the trumpet, or be hungry for bread, and there we will stay" (Jer 42:14). What is both fascinating and disturbing about Jeremiah's story is that Jeremiah himself ends up in Egypt, where he does not want to be, preaching God's word to a people who has chosen its own exile.

The ambiguous nature of the biblical theme of land and the secondary nature of land within the economy of God's relations with his people force us to view place cautiously, even when we are speaking of "stability of place." Nevertheless, in the end, we are forced to acknowledge that place or land is essential within the framework of God's agenda, even if we are merely resident aliens in a land of sojourning.

The Great Commission

If we are going to be informed by the actions of the triune God when we consider the viability of propositions such as a vow of stability, then we must note a frequently discounted element of the Great Commission passage.

> Go therefore and make disciples of all nations, baptizing them in the name of the Father and of the son and of the Holy Spirit, and teaching them to obey everything that I have commanded you. And remember, I am with you always, to the end of the age" (Matt 28:19–20).

It is ironic that a passage many cite to justify a form of "land-loping," often according to individualistic and idiosyncratic visions of "mission," contains Jesus's own vow of stability to his people. In Matthew's gospel, the risen Lord does not ascend as he does in Luke; in Matthew, he is always with his people. Matthew testifies that Jesus is God with us (Matt 1:23), and the Great Commission passage assures us that he will remain with us. Jesus's stability is an expression of God's *ḥesed* Where there is a gathering of God's people, Jesus is present, or as Matthew's Jesus says, "For where two or three are gathered in my name, I am there among them" (Matt 18:20). This is no individualistic vision of stability; instead, it is the risen Christ present to his *ecclesia*. It is divine stability, vowed to the people of God. If it is the case that a primary task of the people of God is to bear witness to our gracious God, then how might we bear witness to his gracious stability? Might our witness to God's stability have an impact even on the way that we read Matthew 28:19–20? How might we conceive of the Great Commission differently if we jettisoned the image of a great Protestant missionary (e.g., William Carey), and instead thought of the Great Commission in terms of the people of God proceeding together to make disciples of all nations? Indeed, what might it mean to understand the baptism into the name of the Father and the Son and the Holy Spirit to be a political act, inducting the baptized into a people who practice a politics that includes *ḥesed, agapē*, and maybe even stability? "[R]emember, I am with you always, to the end of the age" (Matt 28:20).

Jesus, Stability, and the Johannine Corpus

ABIDING

One would be terribly remiss to discuss stability in the New Testament and ignore John 15:1–17:

> I am the true vine, and my Father is the vinegrower. He removes every branch in me that bears no fruit. Every branch that bears fruit he prunes to make it bear more fruit. You have already been cleansed by the word that I have spoken to you. *Abide* in me as I *abide* in you. Just as the branch cannot bear fruit by itself unless it *abides* in the vine, neither can you unless you *abide* in me. I am the vine, you are the branches. Those who *abide* in me and I in them bear much fruit, because apart from me you can do nothing. Whoever does not *abide* in me is thrown away like a branch and withers; such branches are gathered, thrown into the fire, and burned. If you *abide* in me, and my words *abide* in you, ask for whatever you wish, and it will be done for you. My Father is glorified by this, that you bear much fruit and become my disciples. As the Father has loved me, so I have loved you; *abide* in my love. If you keep my commandments, you will *abide* in my love, just as I have kept my Father's commandments and *abide* in his love. I have said these things to you so that my joy may be in you, and that your joy may be complete.
>
> This is my commandment, that you love one another as I have loved you. No one has greater love than this, to lay down one's life for one's friends. You are my friends if you do what I command you. I do not call you servants any longer, because the servant does not know what the master is doing; but I have called you friends, because I have made known to you everything that I have heard from my Father. You did not choose me but I chose you. And I appointed you to go and bear fruit, fruit that will *abide*, so that the father will give you whatever you ask him in my name. I am giving you these commands so that you may love one another. [italics added]

If the disciples of Jesus wish to bear fruit, then they must abide in him as he abides in them. Apart from Jesus, the disciple can do nothing, but if the disciples and Jesus abide together, then all things are possible. What is this fruit? Would it be the Pauline fruit of the Spirit (Gal 5)? Certainly, such things would not be excluded; but I think that the context would suggest that the primary fruit born of abiding with Jesus is *agapē*.[26] Jesus calls for a specific type of imitation from his disciples: "As the Father has loved me, so I have loved you; *abide* in my love. If you keep my commandments, you will *abide* in my love, just as I have kept my Father's commandments and *abide* in his love" (John 15:9–10). The disciples are to follow the commands of Jesus by abiding in his *agapē*. This love's source is the love between the Father and the Son, which spills over into the lives of the disciples who abide in their love.

What is *not* presented here is a private, exclusive love between the lone disciple and Jesus. Rather, we are given a vision of the *agapē*-filled life that is drawn from the true source: the Father's love. The logic is simple: If disciples abide with Jesus, then they are intimately connected with the source of love, like a branch connected to a vine, and the *agapē*-fruit will be born. Without such a connection to the Father's love, the fruit withers. With such a connection, all things are possible and the Father is glorified by our *agapē*. The connection to the vine is essential to the bearing of fruit, but the process of abiding in the vine is not itself equivalent to bearing fruit. In other words, the Christian disciple must abide with Christ as a branch in the vine if the disciple wishes to bear the fruit of *agapē*. But this abiding with Christ is distinct from the bearing of fruit. One can be connected to the vine yet still find oneself removed because no fruit is born. "If you keep my commandments, you will abide in my love" (John 15:10)

"This is my commandment, that you love one another as I have loved you. No one has greater love than this, to lay down one's life for one's friends" (John 15:12–13). We are commissioned, if we would abide in Christ, to love as we have been loved. Employing the earlier analogy of the vine and branches, we might say that as branches of

---

[26] In the following discussion of *agapē* love, I would refer the reader back to the discussion of *agapē* in chapter one.

the true vine, we must bear the fruit of a love, a fruit consistent with the source of the fruit: the love between the Son and the Father.

Yet none of this happens without abiding! This passage asserts that an abiding branch can be removed if it does not bear fruit, but the text also indicates, "whoever does not abide in me is thrown away like a branch and withers" (John 15:6). John presents a dynamic relationship between loving (or bearing fruit) and abiding; each seems to be dependent upon the other because the love of the Father is an abiding love. To abide is to wait patiently, to bear with another, to remain in place. To abide with one another is to dwell or sojourn together. Jesus asks his disciples to abide in him as he has abided in them. Stability with Christ is essential to Christian discipleship and to the bearing of fruit. Abiding with Jesus means abiding in his love as he abides in his Father's love. In John 15, abiding is intimately linked to loving and to proving discipleship. Is it too large of a leap to claim that we are called to let such abiding love spill over into our relationships with one another as the people of God?

1 John

Abiding language and *agapē* language is taken up in one other place in the Johannine corpus: in 1 John. Clearly, the writer of 1 John saw a solid connection between abiding and *agapē*. The writer asserts that a deep connection exists between the "source love" (love between the Father and the Son) and the disciples' love for one another.

> We know love by this, that he laid down his life for us—and we ought to lay down our lives for one another. How does God's love *abide* in anyone who has the world's goods and sees a brother or sister in need yet refuses to help? Little children, let us love, not in word or speech, but in truth and action. . . . And this is his commandment, that we should believe in the name of his Son Jesus Christ and love one another just as he has commanded us. All who obey his commandments *abide* in him, and he abides in them. And by this we know that he abides in us, by the Spirit that he has given us. . . . Beloved, let us love one another because love is from God; everyone who loves is born of God and knows God. Whoever does not love does not know God, for God is love. God's love was revealed among us in this way: God sent his only Son into the world so that we might

live through him. In this is love, not that we loved God but that he loved us and sent his Son to be an atoning sacrifice for our sins. Beloved, since God loved us so much, we also ought to love one another. . . . God is love, and those who *abide* in love *abide* in God, and God *abides* in them . . . We love because he first loved us. Those who say, "I love God," and hate their brothers or sisters are liars; for those who do not love a brother or sister whom they have seen, cannot love God whom they have not seen. The commandment we have from him is this; those who love God must love their brothers and sisters also. (1 John 3:16–18, 23–24; 4:7–11, 16, 19–21) [italics added]

The first epistle of John calls us to embrace the abiding love of God and to incorporate it into our relationships to one another as the people of God. We are called to practice stability.

Rare is the person who has maintained deep ties with Christian brothers and sisters at home and abroad over a long period of time. We have lost the art of abiding Christian friendship in a culture where friendship is often determined by shared commercial interests only to pass away as interests fade or come to completion.

Abiding love demands sacrifice. Stability comes at a cost. It might mean saying no to the higher-paying or higher-status job that is offered and saying yes to staying put. It might mean saying no to an Internet romance, so that you can say yes to the people you worship with. Limited mobility may mean that your children won't get to adhere to Walt Disney's dictum and "follow their dreams."

Abiding love may mean that you have to stand by your brother and sister during those times that friendship becomes most difficult—during betrayal, weakness, depression, or boredom. Abiding love means that you grind away at maintaining relationship even after the thrill is gone. Abiding love may mean that you have to lay down your life for your brother or sister. So often, this is imagined as the sort of love that is willing to "take a bullet for another"; we so often render the gospel irrelevant by hyperbole. Laying down your life for another may be nothing more than setting aside your agendas for personal development and success so that you might lovingly abide with another. Not very sexy is it?

Before moving on from the New Testament, I want to look at one early Christian practice and assess the ways it might bear witness to stability.

Eucharist

We have seen in chapter 1 on vows the importance of covenant for the identity of Israel. By the time of the New Testament, the "covenant," in Judaism, referred to Mosaic law, and, in the Roman Empire, a "covenant" meant an illegal secret society. Separate definitions of *covenant* for Jews and for Romans made it very difficult for Christians to effectively use the term *covenant*. Of the thirty-three references to *covenant* in the New Testament, nearly half are either Old Testament quotations or references to the Old Testament covenants.

Despite these difficulties, we can conclude that early Christians understood themselves, at least for a time, to be a community bound together by covenant. The primary basis for this conclusion is found in the Last Supper narratives (Matt 26:28; Mark 14:24; Luke 22:20; 1 Cor 11:25). In each source, the blood of Jesus Christ is understood to relate to the new covenant, transcending the blood of the old Mosaic covenant (Exod 24:8). In light of Old Testament and ancient Near Eastern covenant forms, there can be little doubt that the practice of the Eucharist was seen as a formal rite by which a covenant relationship was established. It is quite possible that even Gentile converts to Christianity would have seen the Eucharist as some type of covenant-sealing practice. "Since the time of Homer, libations involving a cup of wine were so normal a form of sealing treaties that *spondai* ('libations') became the term for 'treaty.'"[27]

Hence, it is reasonable to assume that, at least in some places, early Christians understood that through baptism and the Eucharist, they were being included in God's new covenant people. Their very participation in the Lord's Supper was, to some degree, a regular renewal of the covenantal binding to the God of Jesus Christ and to one another. The very same God who called Israel to be his unique covenant people had also called them to bear witness to his love and faithfulness, to be a blessing to the nations. Through the practice of the Eucharist, Christians now stand in continuity with the children

[27] Mendenhall, "Covenant," 722.

of Abraham, sharing in the inheritance and in the accompanying responsibility. Christians, too, are people of the covenant.

When we break bread and drink wine together in the presence of God, we are reaffirming our participation in the covenant. This ought to have tremendous implications on our lives. Does one come to the covenantal relationship with everything settled? Or does one come with everything to be redecided? Everything is at stake in this question. Covenant requires a radical break from views of God that vote for untouchable detachment. We often want Gods of power and self-sufficiency who will affirm our own claims for power and self-sufficiency. We do not want the vulnerable God who hangs crucified in the person of Jesus Christ. We do not want a covenanting God who bids us come and drink the cup of the new covenant. We want a God who will stay in heaven.

Our current consumer culture has need of an irrelevant God, for whom nothing is at stake, a kind of indifferent, immune sponsor—whose sole purpose is to affirm our personal dreams. Such a limp god is confronted and destroyed in the claim of covenant. Yahweh sends the consumers scattering with his demand for partnership rather than for commercial exchange. Our personal "plans" are ruined, no longer our own, because Yahweh wants to share in them. Yahweh is terrifying because he calls us to a covenantal vulnerability like his own. There is no immune quarter, no answer in the back of the book, no safe conduct. Only faith. This God prefers steadfast covenant partners with whom things are only decided with deference to our commitments to him and his people. This God is more than willing and able to call our personal dreams and appetites into question; God is forever calling us to a life that embodies the Eucharist. One might speculate that as Christ is present in the Eucharist, so the Eucharist might be present in his people.

Once again, it appears that Benedict's vow of stability complements the biblical vision for our common life. The vow of stability is itself a radical act that brings us into radical vulnerability with one another, a state similar to the vulnerability embodied in the sharing of the Eucharist. Those who share a vow of stability enter into a life that is shared, one that is no longer guided by a single rudder, one that is terrifying to many Americans. It may be possible to say that the vow of stability gives particularistic expression to the vow we participate in when we become members of the new covenant with Jesus. At the least we should be able to assert that the vow of stability sincerely aims to help the people of God live consistently with Yahweh's own means and ends.

One example of these ends and means can be seen in the actual practice of the Eucharist. If the Eucharist is going to be a shared practice that calls us to radical openness to God and to one another, then that Eucharist needs to happen regularly in a certain place. It needs to happen in a place of stability where the participants show up each time to welcome one another and to welcome the stranger and the pilgrim. It is a sad commentary on our church that even in those places that are willing to undertake the weekly practice of Eucharist, it is frequently a Eucharist of strangers. We have forgotten the relevance of Paul's call to "discern the body" (1 Cor 11:29) because we have forgotten the names of those who partake of the elements with us. Stability is essential where the Eucharist is practiced. How can a place offer authentic welcome to the stranger and the pilgrim if all are strangers to one another? Christian hospitality suffers in the absence of stability. Could it be that we have conceded too much to the professional hospitality industry and have lost our vision for Christian hospitality? If so, what might this loss of hospitality say about our Eucharistic practices? If we are going to resist the popularized version of Eucharist as some sort of "magic" transaction between the individual and God,[28] then we are going to have to allow our imaginations to be inspired by the ways that stability and hospitality must be tied to our Eucharistic practices.

One Vision for a New Monastic Vow of Stability

Certainly, the New Testament bears witness to a variety of church orders.[29] What we do see is that the Bible does bear witness to the virtue of stability. Over and against those who would see the vow of stability as some "pharisaic" rule added to the gospel as an appendage of self-justification, we can see that stability is, in fact, a

[28] This is often the way sacramentalist views of the Eucharist get shallowly characterized, though this is a false characterization, which I believe is primarily the product of popular misunderstanding.

[29] See especially Schweizer, *Church Order in the New Testament*.

faithful attempt to embody Scripture. As people of a covenanting God who practices justice and/or righteousness along with steadfast *agapē*, we are called to imitate our God. The vow of stability is one form of legitimate imitation. Stability as a form of God-imitation is not without its failings (but all forms of God-imitation are touched by human failure.). Nevertheless, stability is legitimate imitation. In light of the biblical witness, we might find it fruitful to ask ourselves, why not undertake such a vow?

I am a member of an intentional community that makes a vow of stability. We call it our Statement of Commitment. It reads as follows:

> We come together as single followers of our Lord and Savior, Jesus Christ. In response to the promptings of His Spirit we are determined to seek first His kingdom, ordering our lives by its values and submitting to His lordship through this local expression of His body. By this statement we express our covenant with one another under the lordship of Jesus Christ.
>
> It is our desire to live out life in listening response to His call. Where He calls us to love one another, we shall, learning from Him and from each other the art of loving. Where He calls us to servanthood, we shall humbly offer ourselves. Where He urges us to become holy as He is holy, we will abandon the false pursuits of the world and will receive thankfully the correction of our sister and brother. We affirm that our confession of Christ means that we will live out our discipleship in union with others, that together we are His body, that the church is God's tool for accomplishing His objective in the world. Together, we wish to be a light to the world showing His love.
>
> Because of this and my desire to grow up into true servanthood, recognizing that light is discovered only when I choose not to claim life for myself, I give my life away, no longer living for me but living for you. I abandon my destiny to the Lord. Knowing His Spirit works through His people, I share with you the control of that destiny. Short of a violation of my conscience, as it is purified through the church, I will defer to the voice of the church and its gifts as it speaks to my life. My commitment to you is that I will not seek to leave without a call from God that has been confirmed by

this body. I trust that you will honor me as part of your family and not take my offering lightly.

I accept you as my sisters and brothers and promise to cherish the gift of our relationship. I will strive for our unity by praying for you, helping you, serving you, and forgiving you. I ask you to care for me, to encourage me to love and good works, to call me on when you see me falling away, and to stand beside me in my struggle.

Now, then, we are one body. We are born of one Spirit and seek strength from one source. We shall be together for as long as God allows. We rejoice in our unity, a gift of our Father. And we go forth, together, in His service.

Authentic community takes time. Like anything of value, it comes at a cost. Our culture of immediate reward and gratification resists this truth in the interest of consumerism. We enter into this vow that we have named our Statement of Commitment in order to counterculturally identify with Yahweh, in order to bear witness to the God of Jesus Christ. We make promises and keep them; we enter into a vow of stability.

Our primary concern in the making of this vow is with the creation of a *polis* that is shaped by the character of God as revealed in Jesus and the Scriptures. We desire a *polis* that is held together by obedience to God. Yet we so often fail (Hos 4:1; Jer 25:31). Thank God that his loyalty is greater than our own, and that we find forgiveness in it. Our covenants form the social function of creating a particular type of stability (e.g., marriage covenants). Is it even possible to form a "place" or "community" fragrant with God's *shalom* without entering into such vows? We have always answered this question with a "No!" And so, all members mutually affirm the Statement of Commitment, one to another. We share our vow before God, allowing him to be party to it.

Agreements between individuals before a deity were common in the ancient Near East. But the Israelite covenant is entirely different from other Near Eastern agreements. With the covenant between Yahweh and Israel, an entire people enters into a covenant with its God and orders its common life accordingly. Hence, righteousness among God's Hebrew people primarily means doing those things that maintain the covenant. Sin is that which transgresses the covenant. The covenantal obligations are summed up in the word *ḥesed*.

I spoke at length about *ḥesed* in chapter 1, yet these words from G. Ernest Wright help to summarize our communal understanding as Church of the Servant King:

> No member of the community can do as he pleases. He must be loyal to his covenanted obligations; that is, he must exercise *ḥesed*, involving obedience to the Divine commandments which are the laws of the community, a proper reverence (fear) for God, and justice and kindness toward his fellowmen. God, on the other hand, will keep His part of the covenant by exercising or "showing" *ḥesed* toward His people; that is, He will bring help and redemption to them, will be loyal to His promises to them, and will be righteous and merciful.[30]

Shalom and *berith* ("covenant") are practically synonymous. *Shalom* refers to the state of those who participate in the harmonious society. *Berith* refers to the community and all the privileges and obligations that community implies. Covenant and *shalom* go hand in hand; God's community must have one to experience the other.

Our culture has long suffered from individualism gone wild. We often conceive of ourselves primarily as individuals, who have the right to do whatever we wish without hindrance. For Americans, this individualism implies a right to consumer choice; our national *polis* seems to have been more and more to reduced to a *polis* of consumption (undergirded by a violence that maintains our privilege to consume). Yet, no one lives in a vacuum; no man is an island; we were not created to consume. We are created by God for community. The question remains, for what sort of community? One answer to this question has been offered in the Statement of Commitment. Our own personal crisis may come answering the question of what sort of community currently holds our allegiance.

> The self-centered individual is inclined to think mainly of himself and his own salvation. But one who stands humbly in the fear of the Lord understands also our corporate responsibility before God. Man must ever be concerned with the ideal society, with the Kingdom on earth, with "the covenant of peace," else he is disobedient to his heavenly vision.

[30] Wright, *Challenge*, 91.

> In the last tragic hours of His life Jesus fastened on Jeremiah's ideal and spoke of "the new covenant in My blood," thus binding Himself and the Christian community together and to God. From that day to this when Christian people have celebrated the Lord's supper, they have reaffirmed their adherence to the covenant bond which unites them to God in "the blood" of Jesus Christ.[31]

As Church of the Servant King, we have traditionally seen our Statement of Commitment as our attempt to articulate the social expression of the new covenant that has been written on our hearts at baptism. At one time, our community occasionally called this the Covenant Statement because it was the statement that we shared with one another at our annual covenant retreat. The name "Covenant Statement" is misleading, however, because we do not see the Statement of Commitment as a covenant that is additional to the new covenant. Like the vast majority of followers in historic Christianity, we see that the new covenant is fully sufficient. We make our statement of commitment to one another not to improve on the new covenant in any way but rather to help us recognize the social, promissory, and local elements of the gospel.

Our Statement of Commitment serves as an expression to the promises or vows that we make upon membership in the Church of the Servant King. The document is no more than an attempt to give concrete expression to the nature of our membership to one another in Christ. It was not handed down to us from God; it is not some new Torah; it does not cover every possibility that might arise in our ecclesial life. Our Statement of Commitment does not exercise authority in and of itself; it does not function as Scripture. Rather, it is merely our attempt to articulate the social, promissory, and local nature of the gospel.

Congruent with the language of *polis* is the language of *place*. Another document that has been circulated in our twentieth-anniversary booklet, in our Christian education classes, and in an Ekklesia Project seminar is a document that attempts to speak of our life and mission creating a particular type of "place." Unless we remain together, so much of what we hope for in this place will go unrealized. Our articulation of place follows:

[31] Ibid., 98.

A Place Where Life Is Laid Down
for the Sake of God's Kingdom

We are trying to be an authentic witness to the nature of our Lord Jesus Christ. God has called us to follow his example and set aside "life" (aspirations, pleasure, health, rest, safety, family, image, respect, dreams) for the sake of his kingdom and for the sake of the other. With the help of the Spirit, we are committed to following this example.

> Then Jesus told his disciples, "If any man would come after me, let him deny himself and take up his cross and follow me. For whoever would save his life will lose it, and whoever loses his life for my sake will find it. For what will it profit a man, if he gains the whole world and forfeits his life? Or what shall a man give in return for his life?" (Matt 16:24–26)

A Place of Reconciliation and Forgiveness

We are trying to be an authentic witness to the nature of our Lord Jesus Christ. God has called us to follow his example: to extend forgiveness and to participate in reconciliation as God has done in Jesus. With the help of the Spirit, we are committed to following this example.

> Holy Father, keep them in thy name, which thou hast given me, that they may be one, even as we are one. (John 17:11)

A Place of Hospitality

We are trying to be an authentic witness to the nature of our Lord Jesus Christ. God has called us to follow his example: to create a place of welcome and rest as he does, to be generous as he is, to welcome the stranger as he does. With the help of the Spirit, we are committed to following this example.

> Do not neglect to show hospitality to strangers, for thereby some have entertained angels unawares. (Heb 13:2)

A Place of Discipleship and Transformation

We are trying to be an authentic witness to the nature of our Lord Jesus Christ. We follow a God who wants to see us grow up. We follow a God who nurtures and challenges, disciplines and comforts, so that we might be found "holy and acceptable." With the help of the Spirit, we are committed to following this example.

> I appeal to you therefore, brethren, by the mercies of God, to present your bodies as a living sacrifice, holy and acceptable to God, which is your spiritual worship. do not be conformed to this world but be transformed by the renewal of your mind, that you may prove what is the will of God, what is good and acceptable and perfect. (Rom 12:1–2)

> And his gifts were that some should be apostles, some prophets, some evangelists, some pastors and teachers, for the equipment of the saints, for the work of ministry, for the building up the body of Christ, until we all attain the unity of the faith and of the knowledge of the Son of God, to mature manhood, to the measure of the stature of the fullness of Christ; so that we may no longer be children, tossed to and fro and carried about with every wind of doctrine, by the cunning of men, by their craftiness in deceitful wiles. Rather, speaking the truth in love, we are to grow up in every way into him who is the head, into Christ, from whom the whole body, joined and knit together by every joint with which it is supplied, when each part is working properly, makes bodily growth and upbuilds itself in love. (Eph 4:11–16)

A Place of Gratitude, Joy, and Celebration

We are trying to be an authentic witness to the nature of our Lord Jesus Christ. God has called us to follow his example: Yahweh is king among the other gods when it comes to joy and celebration; Bacchus's party spirit pales in comparison with the joy of Yahweh. Yahweh is alone among the gods when it comes to expressing gratitude. Expressed most clearly in the life of Christ, God's gratitude is a virtue that lies at the heart of the Trinity. With the help of the Spirit, we are committed to following this example.

Make a joyful noise to the Lord, all the lands! Serve the Lord with gladness! Come into his presence with singing! Know that the Lord is God! It is he that made us, and we are his; we are his people, and the sheep of his pasture. Enter his gates with thanksgiving, and his courts with praise! Give thanks to him, bless his name! For the Lord is good; his steadfast love endures for ever, and his faithfulness to all generations. (Psalm 100)

A Place of Service

We are trying to be an authentic witness to the nature of our Lord Jesus Christ. God has called us to follow his example: Jesus came not to be served but to serve. With the help of the spirit, we are committed to following this example.

Come, O blessed of my Father, inherit the kingdom prepared for you from the foundation of the world; for I was hungry and you gave me food, I was thirsty and you gave me drink, I was a stranger and you welcomed me, I was naked and you clothed me, I was sick and you visited me, I was in prison and you came to me. (Matt 25:34–36)

A Place of Steadfast Love, Fellowship, and Belonging

We are trying to be an authentic witness to the nature of our Lord Jesus Christ. God has called us to follow his example: Yahweh is the God of dogged love and steadfast loyalty. Yahweh is fellowship, this is expressed most clearly in the truth of the Trinity. Yahweh has by grace allowed us to belong to him. With the help of the Spirit, we are committed to following this example.

Therefore, since we are surrounded by so great a cloud of witnesses, let us also lay aside every weight, and sin which clings so closely, and let us run with perseverance the race that is set before us, looking to Jesus the pioneer and perfecter of our faith, who for the joy that was set before him endured the cross, despising the shame, and is seated at the right hand of the throne of God. (Heb 12:1–3)

Our Statement of Commitment and this vision of "place" compliment one another in giving a clear expression of the mission and ministry of Church of the Servant King. As any reader of Wendell

Berry knows (and there are many among us), the creation of a particular type of place on this earth requires habits of stability.

Nevertheless, we resist attempting to see stability as our own doing. Our social fabric, our communal testimony, is held together primarily through the gifts of the Spirit. The Holy Spirit is comforter, challenger, animator, and sustainer of our common life.

Promise also plays a vitally important role in the sustaining of our community, primarily because we trust in and depend upon the promises of God. Our God is, without a doubt, a promise-making and promise-keeping God. Yahweh enters into agreements and upholds his covenants. God's word is true. That Yahweh is the God of dogged love and steadfast loyalty bears repeating.

What role do our own vows or promises play in our being the Church of the Servant King? How important are our own promises in God's economy? These questions bring us back to the Statement of Commitment. Each year, we stand in a circle and recite this commitment to one another. What is so important about such an act?

1. Maintaining our commitment, keeping our promises, remembering our vows, must not be taken lightly, for they bear testimony to the nature of our God.

2. Maintaining our commitment, keeping our promises, our remembering our vows, must not be taken lightly, for the trustworthiness of our word is essential to the maintenance of our social fabric. In other words, in order to create the type of place that we believe we are called to, we must be able to trust one another.

3. Maintaining our commitment, keeping our promises, remembering our vows, is essential, most of all, because they are made before God. The promise is made in the context of one another but is made in relation to God. We take with utmost seriousness this yearly repetition of our vows before one another and before God because a trusting, loving relationship with God is the foundation of our life together and of our service to God in this world.

Obviously, it would be absurd to attempt to claim that such a vow as we make as Church of the Servant King is essential for all

Christians at all times. Nevertheless, the people of God must accept the challenge to give some kind of concrete expression that bears an authentic witness to God and the gospel. Like Benedict in his time and place, we have found a vow of stability to be essential for our particular common life. The creation of a particular *polis* requires particular common practices. The ideas of *shalom* and covenant compliment one another intimately. It is impossible for those of us in community to imagine our commitment to the type of place we want to be, without our commitment to stability.

Like all good things, the vow of stability can be abused and misused. If space allowed, I could say some about this as well. Yet, despite any dangers from abuse or misuse of our vows (and we have experienced some of these dangers in our common life), this essay is offered to encourage communities of the new monasticism to consider implementing a vow of stability, a piece of the Christian witness from historic monasticism.

Conclusion

IN HER ESSAY "RULE and Gospel: Meaning of Benedictine Vowing," Sister Mary Collins argues that obedience, the monastic way of life, and stability find their center "in Christ."[1] In and of themselves, there is nothing particularly Christian about a commitment to do what another says, to live by a rule, or to stay in one place—which is a way of saying that these are secondary commitments. They serve some greater purpose. For Benedictines, the threefold promise serves the purpose of rooting a community's life in Christ. Obedience to an abbot or abbess is obedience to the command of Christ. But that command is not meted out in decrees from on high. It is conditioned by a way of life—a commitment on the part of every community member (including the abbess) to always be turning toward God. Ironically, this commitment to be changed is what makes stability necessary. Stability is a commitment to abide in Christ. It is to stick with the way of conversion. It is to listen to one's superior. Stability is conversion is obedience. In Christ, the three become one way of life.

We noted in our introduction to this book that Benedictines insist on the unity of their threefold promise. Because Jesus Christ is the fulfillment of Israel, we believe that the unity of the threefold promise in Christ is also true of God's people in the context of covenant relationship. What is more, saying it this way helps us to see why the threefold promise requires a people.

The importance of land for Israel is fundamentally about stability. God's covenant relationship with Israel needs a place to happen. So God brings Israel up out of Egypt and into the Promised Land. God even drives out the other nations, not so much because Israel alone has "divine right" to the land, but because God's people are in need of conversion from the way of life that other peoples live. (And as long as those other peoples are around, God's people are tempted

[1] See Collins, "Rule and Gospel."

to chase after their gods.) The law is a gift meant to show Israel the way that leads to life. But it can only be received by faith—a faith that requires obedience. God's people must follow God's way even when it looks like that will mean their death. The story of Gideon's army in Judges 7 is a good example of the obedience God desires of Israel. In this story, the people (as an army) obey the Lord, trust the way that God gives them (even though it looks like they'll be wiped out), and receive the land where they will dwell with God. Obedience, conversion, and stability are one in service to God's covenant with Israel.

If the new monasticism movement is to be of any service to the kingdom of God, it must find ways to root itself in Christ and in God's covenant with Israel. We believe that the threefold promise of obedience, conversion, and stability may help us to find these roots. We've tried to show in this book how this threefold promise has been helpful for us free-church Protestants trying to live the new monasticism.

It is with caution and some trepidation that we call new monasticism a "movement." We do not trust movements. To quote farmer and poet Wendell Berry,

> People in movements . . . too easily become unable to mean their own language, as when a "peace movement" becomes violent. They often become too specialized, as if finally they cannot help taking refuge in the pinhole vision of the institutional intellectuals. They almost always fail to be radical enough, dealing finally in effects rather than causes. Or they deal with single issues or single solutions, as if to assure themselves that they will not be radical enough.[2]

Movements that are rooted in nothing more than the mass-produced feelings of the culture will no doubt move on. But it is also true that God sometimes moves among the people called church to re-create a way of life together. No one controls such movements. They are always a gift from God. If, indeed, we have been caught up in a movement worthy of the name "new monasticism," we pray that God will give us wisdom to learn from Scripture and the church's long tradition how to live faithfully in such a time as this.

---

[2] Berry, "In Distrust of Movements," 14–16.

We pray this not only for ourselves and for our communities but for the whole church. While these reflections certainly come from and are meant for communities like ours, we trust they have something to say to the church as a whole. Monastic communities have long been places of study where books have been written for the edification of all God's people. We hope this book will become a small contribution to that tradition.

But we also know from experience that there are people in America who, disappointed by what they have seen and heard from churches, are nevertheless intrigued by what they hear about Jesus and about his followers who have left everything through the ages to follow his way of life and peace. Many of our communities have become places of seeking for folks like this—whether agnostic, Jewish, Muslim, or Buddhist. While this book has certainly been a Christian reflection on life in Christian communities, we believe that Jesus and his way are good news for the whole world. So we hope this volume will also add to the rich conversation and friendships we share with non-Christians.

Time magazine recently ran a cover story titled "Does God Want You To Be Rich?"[3] The article focused on Joel Osteen, pastor of the fastest-growing church in America, and his "new gospel of wealth." This is not the old "name-it-and-claim-it" prosperity gospel of the 1980s televangelists. Less dramatic and more pragmatic, the new gospel of wealth simply claims that God wants to bless his children with material prosperity in this present age. It may take sacrifice and it may take time, but God is in the "blessing business." Jesus Christ empowers people to achieve the American dream.

Toward the end of the article, the authors note that not all Christians believe that the favor of the Lord resembles middle-class success. Not the "New Monastics," they write, identifying us as a "sprinkling of Protestant groups . . . experimenting with the kind of communal living that has previously been the province of Catholic orders."[4] We believe we have heard a gospel different from the gospel of wealth that is, indeed, in keeping with the news that the Catholic orders have proclaimed and practiced through the centuries. While this gospel is, like the new gospel of wealth, concerned with the here

[3] See Van Biema and Chu, "Does God," 48–56.
[4] Ibid., 56.

and now, it turns the success of the American dream on its head. God wants a new social order to come on earth as it is in heaven.

"Whoever wishes to become great among you must become your servant," Jesus says, "and whoever wishes to be first among you must be the slave of all" (Mark 10:43–44). The good news isn't that you're OK and we're OK, but that God can convert us all into the people we were made to be in community. The good news isn't that we have all the answers, but that we can submit to a wisdom greater than ourselves and find peace in a new way of life. The good news isn't that you can go anywhere and do anything, but that you are free to stay where you are and grow up with God's people into the full stature of Christ.

In the end our prayer is that this book and our lives in community may somehow point to the true gospel in a world that is full of false gospels and people who are dying for lack of good news. We pray that you will hear and believe—and join us in the adventure of inhabiting the church.

Abbreviations

ATANT   Abhandlungen zur Theologie des Alten und Neuen Testaments

CC   Continental Commentaries

IBC   Interpretation: A Biblical Commentary for Teaching and Preaching

IDB   *The Interpreter's Dictionary of the Bible.* Edited by G. A. Buttrick. 4 vols. Nashville: Abingdon, 1962.

NICNT   New International Commentary on the New Testament

NIGTC   New International Greek Testament Commentary

P   Prologue to the *Rule of St. Benedict*

RB   *Rule of St. Benedict*

Bibliography

Anderson, Bernhard W. *The Eighth-Century Prophets: Amos, Hosea, Isaiah, Micah.* 1978. Reprinted, Eugene, OR: Wipf & Stock, 2003.

Anderson, John. "On Becoming an Apache or What It Means to Become the People of God." *The Other Side* (Nov. 1, 1998).

Alt, Albrecht. "The God of the Fathers." In *Essays on Old Testament History and Religion,* 1–77. Translated by R. A. Wilson. Oxford: Blackwell, 1966.

Arnold, Eberhard. "Why We Live in Community." In *Why We Live in Community,* 1–32. 3d ed. New York: Plough, 1995.

Augustine. *The Confessions.* Translated by Maria Boulding. New York: Vintage, 1998.

Baltzer, Klaus. *The Covenant Formulary: In Old Testament, Jewish, and Early Christian Writings.* Translated by David E. Green. Philadelphia: Fortress, 1971.

Barth, Karl. *The Word of God and the Word of Man.* Translated with a new foreword by Douglas Horton. New York: Harper, 1957.

Bartholomew, Craig, and Thorston Moritz, editors. *Christ and Consumerism: Critical Reflections on the Spirit of Our Age.* Carlisle: Paternoster, 2000.

Bellah, Robert, et al. *Habits of the Heart: Individualism and Commitment in American Life.* Berkeley: University of California Press, 1985.

Benson, Bruce Ellis. "Tearing Down the Wall: Rethinking the Relation of Artist and Community." *Mars Hill Review* 23 (2004) 45–56.

Berry, Wendell. "In Distrust of Movements." *Resurgence* 198 (2000) 14–16.

Beaudoin, Tom. *Consuming Faith: Integrating Who We Are with What We Buy.* Lanham, MD: Sheed and Ward, 2003.

Boesak, Allan A. *Farewell to Innocence: A Social-Ethical Study on Black Theology and Black Power.* Maryknoll, NY: Orbis, 1977.

Bonhoeffer, Dietrich. *Life Together.* Translated with an introduction by John W. Doberstein. San Francisco: Harper San Francisco, 1993.

———. *Life Together; Prayerbook of the Bible,* edited by Geffrey B. Kelly. Translated by Daniel W. Bloesch and James H. Burtness. Dietrich Bonhoeffer Works 5. Minneapolis: Fortress, 1996.

Brueggemann, Walter. *The Land: Place as Gift, Promise, and Challenge in Biblical Faith.* 2d ed. Philadelphia: Fortress, 2002.

———. *Genesis.* IBC. Atlanta: John Knox, 1982.

———. "Covenant as a Subversive Paradigm." In *A Social Reading of the Old Testament: Prophetic Approaches to Israel's Communal Life,* edited by Patrick D. Miller, 43–53. Philadelphia: Fortress, 1994.

———. *Theology of the Old Testament: Testimony, Dispute, Advocacy.* Minneapolis: Fortress, 1997.

Bibliography

Burton-Christie, Douglas. *Scripture and the Quest for Holiness in Early Christian Monasticism.* New York: Oxford University Press, 1993.

Byasee, Jason. "The New Monastics: Alternative Christian Communities." *Christian Century* (Oct. 18, 2005) 38–47.

Casey, Michael. *An Unexciting Life: Reflections on Benedictine Spirituality.* Petersham, MA: St. Bede's, 2005.

Cassidy, John. "Me Media." *The New Yorker* (May 15, 2006) 50–59.

Cavanaugh, William T. "Killing for the Telephone Company: Why the Nation-State is Not the Keeper of the Common Good." *Modern Theology* 20 (2004) 243–74.

Chittister, Joan. *Wisdom Distilled from the Daily: Living the Rule of St. Benedict Today.* San Francisco: HarperSanFrancisco, 1991.

Chitty, Derwas J. *The Desert a City: An Introduction to Egyptian and Palestian Monasticism under the Christian Empire.* Crestwood, NY: St. Vladimir's Seminary Press, 1995.

Clapp, Rodney. "The Theology of Consumption and the Consumption of Theology: Toward a Christian Response to Consumerism." In *The Consuming Passion: Christianity and the Consumer Culture,* edited by Rodney Clapp, 169–204. Downers Grove, IL: InterVarsity, 1998.

Collins, Mary. "Rule and Gospel: The Meaning of Benedictine Vowing." *Benedictines* 35 (1980) 27–46.

Cistercian Order of the Strict Observance. *Constitutions and Statutes of the Cistercian Order of the Strict Observance.* "Stability of Place." http://www.ocso.org/cst-stat/cc-m-en.htm.

Dawn, Marva J. *Unfettered Hope: A Call to Faithful Living in an Affluent Society.* Louisville: Westminster John Knox, 2003.

Dodd, C. H. *The Bible and the Greeks.* London: Hodder and Stoughton, 1935.

Dunn, Marilyn. *The Emergence of Monasticism: From the Desert Fathers to the Early Middle Ages.* Oxford: Blackwell, 2000.

Eichrodt, Walter. *Theology of the Old Testament.* Translated by J. A. Baker. 2 vols. Old Testament Library. Philadelphia: Westminster 1961–1967.

Fishbane, Michael. *Biblical Interpretation in Ancient Israel.* Oxford: Clarendon, 1985.

Glueck, Nelson. *Ḥesed in the Bible.* Translated by Alfred Gottschalk, with an introduction by Gerald A. Larue. Edited by Elias L. Epstein. Cincinnati: Hebrew Union College Press, 1967.

Grosheide, F. W. *Commentary on the First Epistle to the Corinthians.* NICNT. Grand Rapids: Eerdmans, 1953.

Hafiz, Mohammad Shams od-Din. "Let's Eat." In *The Gift: Poems by the Great Sufi Master.* Translated by Daniel James Ladinsky. New York: Arkana, 1999.

Hauerwas, Stanley. *A Better Hope: Resources for a Church Confronting Capitalism, Democracy, and Postmodernity.* Grand Rapids: Brazos, 2000.

Hallie, Philip P. "How Goodness Happened Here." In *Lest Innocent Blood Be Shed: The Story of the Village of Le Chambon and How Goodness Happened There,* 269–87. New York: Harper Perennial, 1994.

Halteman-Schrok, Jennifer. *Just Eating?: Practicing Our Faith at the Table: Readings for Reflection and Action.* 2 vols. Louisville: Presbyterian Hunger Program, 2005.

Hays, Richard B. *First Corinthians.* IBC. Louisville: John Knox, 1997.

Héring, Jean. *The First Epistle of Saint Paul to the Corinthians.* Translated by A. W. Heathcote and P. J. Allcock. London: Epworth, 1962.

Hunkeler, Leodegar. *It Began with Benedict: The Benedictines, Their Background, Founder, History, Life, Contributions to Church and World.* Translated by Luke Eberle. St. Benedict, OR: Mount Angel Abbey, 1978.

Kant, Immanuel. "Lectures on the Philosophical Doctrine of Religion." In *Religion and Rational Theology.* Translated and edited by Allen W. Wood and George di Giovanni, 335–452. The Cambridge Edition of the Works of Immanuel Kant. Cambridge: Cambridge University Press, 1996.

Kardong, Terrence G. *Benedict's Rule: A Translation and Commentary.* Collegeville, MN: Liturgical, 1981.

Kellenberger, Edgar. håsåd wǎʾåmåt *als ausdruck einer Glaubenserfahrung.* ATANT 69. Zurich: Theologischer Verlag, 1982.

Kierkegaard, Søren. *Purity of Heart is to Will One Thing: Spiritual Preparation for the Office of Confession.* Rev. ed. Translated by Douglas V. Steere. New York: Harper, 1948.

Knowles, David. *Christian Monasticism.* World University Library. New York: McGraaw-Hill, 1969.

LaCocque, André. *Ruth.* Translated by K. C. Hanson. Continental Commentaries. Minneapolis: Fortress, 2004.

Leclercq, Jean. *Aspects of Monasticism.* Translated by Mary Dodd. Kalamazoo, MI: Cistercian, 1978.

Lohfink, Gerhard. "The Torah as Social Project." In *Does God Need the Church?,* 74–87. Translated by Linda M. Maloney. Collegeville, MN: Liturgical, 1999.

MacIntyre, Alasdair. *After Virtue: A Study in Moral Theory.* 2d ed. Notre Dame: University of Notre Dame Press, 1984.

Malina, Bruce J. *The New Testament World: Insights from Cultural Anthropology.* 3d ed. Louisville: Westminster John Knox, 2001.

Marsh, Charles. *The Beloved Community: How Faith Shapes Social Justice, from the Civil Rights Movement to Today.* New York: Basic, 2005.

McDaniel, Jay B. *Living from the Center: Spirituality in an Age of Consumerism.* St. Louis: Chalice, 2000.

McGill, Arthur C. *Death and Life: An American Theology.* Philadelphia: Fortress 1987.

Meisel, Anthony C., and M. L. del Maestro, translators. *The Rule of St. Benedict.* Garden City, NY: Image, 1975.

Mendenhall, George E. *Law and Covenant in Israel and the Ancient Near East.* Pittsburgh: Biblical Colloquium, 1955.

———. "Covenant." In *IBD* 1:714–23.

Merriam-Webster Online. http://www.m-w.com.

Merton, Thomas. *The Sign of Jonas.* New York: Image, 1956.

———. "Building Communities on God's Love." In *Why We Live in Community,* by Eberhard Arnold. 3d ed. 33–52. New York: Plough, 1995.

Moll, Rob. "The New Monasticism." *Christianity Today* (September 2, 2005) 38–46.

Otto, Tim. "Praying is Believing." *Rutba House Newsletter*. Volume 3. Issue 4.

Potok, Chaim. *My Name Is Asher Lev*. New York: Anchor, 1972.

Rutba House, editors. *School(s) for Conversion: Twelve Marks of the New Monasticism*. Eugene, OR: Cascade, 2005.

Sakenfeld, Katharine Doob. *The Meaning of Hesed in the Hebrew Bible: A New Inquiry*. 1978. Reprinted, Eugene, OR: Wipf & Stock, 2002.

———. *Faithfulness in Action: Loyalty in Biblical Perspective*. 1985. Reprinted, Eugene, OR: Wipf & Stock, 2001.

Schaff, Philip, editor. *Saint Chrysostom: Homilies on the Epistles of Paul to the Corinthians*. NPNF 12. Whitefish, MT: Kessinger, 2004.

Schut, Michael, editor and compiler. *Simpler Living, Compassionate Life: A Christian Perspective*. Denver: Living the Good News, 1999.

Schweizer, Eduard. *Church Order in the New Testament*. 1961. Reprinted, Eugene, OR: Wipf & Stock, 2006.

Sider, Ronald J. *The Scandal of the Evangelical Conscience*. Grand Rapids: Baker, 2005.

Shelley, Percy Bysshe. *The Complete Poetry of Percy Bysshe Shelley*. Vol. 2. Edited by Donald H. Reiman, and Neil Fraistat. Baltimore: Johns Hopkins University Press, 2005.

Sitzia, Macrina. "The Benedictine Vow 'Conversio Morum.'" In *Religious Conversion: Contemporary Practices and Controversies*, edited by Christopher Lamb and M. Darrol Bryant, 220–32. London: Cassell, 1999.

Smith, Christian, Michael Emerson, et al. *American Evangelicalism: Embattled and Thriving*. Chicago: University of Chicago Press, 1998.

Smith, Christian. *Christian America? What Evangelicals Really Want*. Berkeley: University of California Press, 2000.

Snyder, John R. "Translator's Introduction." In *The End of Modernity: Nihilism and Hermeneutics in Postmodern Culture*, by Gianni Vattimo, vi–il. Translated by John R. Snyder. Parallax: Re-visions of Culture and Society. Baltimore: Johns Hopkins University Press, 1988.

Thiselton, Anthony C. *The First Epistle to the Corinthians: A Commentary on the Greek Text*. NIGTC. Grand Rapids: Eerdmans, 2000.

Van Biema, David, and Jeff Chu. "Does God Want You to Be Rich?" *Time* (September 18, 2006) 48–56.

Verheyen, Boniface, translator. *The Most Holy Rule of Our Holy Father Benedict*. Available at http://www.monaschos.net/monasticism/benedict/rule.shtml.

Webster, John. *Holiness*. Grand Rapids: Eerdmans, 2003.

Westermann, Claus. *The Promise to the Fathers: Studies on the Patriarchal Narratives*. Translated by David E. Green. Philadelphia: Fortress, 1980.

Wilson, Jonathan R. *Living Faithfully in a Fragmented World: Lessons from Alasdair MacIntyre's "After Virtue."* Harrisburg, PA: Trinity, 1997.

Wilson-Hartgrove, Jonathan. *To Baghdad and Beyond: How I Got Born Again in Babylon*. Eugene, OR: Cascade, 2005.

Witherington, Ben. *Conflict and Community in Corinth: A Socio-Rhetorical Commentary on 1 and 2 Corinthians*. Grand Rapids: Eerdmans, 1995.

Wolff, Hans Walter. *Hosea.* Translated by Gary Stansell. Hermeneia. Philadelphia: Fortress, 1974.

Wolter, Maurus. *Principles of Monasticism.* Translated by Bernard A. Sause. St. Louis: Herder, 1962.

Workman, Herbert B. *The Evolution of the Monastic Ideal.* London: Epworth, 1913.

Wright, G. Ernest. *The Challenge of Israel's Faith.* Chicago: University of Chicago Press, 1944.

Wright, N. T. "Justification and the Church." In *What Saint Paul Really Said: Was Paul of Tarsus the Real Founder of Christianity?*, 113–34. Grand Rapids: Eerdmans, 1997.